THE RELIGION VIRUS

First published by O-Books, 2010
O Books is an imprint of John Hunt Publishing Ltd., The Bothy, Deershot Lodge, Park Lane, Ropley,
Hants, SO24 0BE, UK
office1@o-books.net
www.o-books.net

Distribution in:

UK and Europe
Orca Book Services Ltd
tradeorders@orcabookservices.co.uk
directorders@orcabookservices.co.uk
Tel: 01235 465521 Fax: 01235 465555
Int. code (44)

USA and Canada
NBN
custserv@nbnbooks.com
Tel: 1 800 462 6420 Fax: 1 800 338 4550

Australia and New Zealand
Brumby Books
sales@brumbybooks.com.au
Tel: 61 3 9761 5535 Fax: 61 3 9761 7095

Far East (offices in Singapore, Thailand,
Hong Kong, Taiwan)
Pansing Distribution Pte Ltd
kemal@pansing.com
Tel: 65 6319 9939 Fax: 65 6462 5761

South Africa
Stephan Phillips (pty) Ltd
Email: orders@stephanphillips.com
Tel: 27 21 4489839 Telefax: 27 21 4479879

Text copyright Craig A. James 2009

Design: Craig A. James

ISBN: 978 1 84694 272 3

A CIP catalogue record for this book is available
from the British Library.

Printed by Digital Book Print

O Books operates a distinctive and ethical publishing philosophy in
all areas of its business, from its global network of authors to
production and worldwide distribution.

THE RELIGION VIRUS

WHY YOU BELIEVE IN GOD:
AN EVOLUTIONIST EXPLAINS RELIGION'S
TENACIOIUS HOLD ON HUMANITY

CRAIG A. JAMES

Table of Contents

1. Why is Religion Like an Elephant's DNA?

Abraham's God

He was a wise man who invented God.
– Plato

Most modern Christians, Jews and Muslims would be quite surprised to learn that the Yahweh worshipped by Abraham (also called *El*, *Elohim* and *Jehovah*) was quite different than the almighty God we know today. Abraham's God was made of flesh-and-blood. He was a god of war, jealous and vengeful, more than ready to commit genocide, wipe out humanity with a flood, and many other deeds that made him quite the opposite of the loving, Almighty God we know today. Abraham would have a hard time believing that his Lord and the modern God Almighty are one and the same.

Not only that, but Abraham, as well as all of his descendants down to Moses' time and even beyond, were *polytheists*, that is, pagans. To them, Yahweh was just one god among many. There were so many other gods competing for (and getting) their attention that Yahweh had to make a special deal with them: He offered his military protection, and in return the Israelites had to forgo their other gods and worship only Yahweh. In the days of Abraham, Yahweh simply didn't command the same unquestioned loyalty that He does today.

The loving, omnipotent, fatherly God we learn about today is the result of the longest and best "marketing makeover" in history – four thousand years of changes and improvements to Yahweh's image, from Abraham's time to today. Yahweh has evolved into the Almighty God, the God of everything, the loving, forgiving God, the *only* God. The Yahweh makeover is so complete that we just call him "God" now, with a capital "G". We don't have to distinguish God from the other gods, because most Westerners are monotheists. Yahweh completely dominates Western religions. The other gods that Abraham and Moses believed in are either forgotten, or are grouped together under the dismissive title "mythology."

How did this happen? Did someone in Abraham's time, or Moses' time, realize that Yahweh had an "image problem" that needed polishing up? How did Yahweh change from Abraham's god-of-armies into our God Almighty?

Religious scholars might tell us that Yahweh was always the God we know today, that only our understanding of God has changed. Noah, Abraham, and Moses lived in simpler times, so God presented himself to them in a simpler way, one they could understand. Over the millennia, as our societies and culture matured, God was able to reveal more and more of his all-knowing, loving, all-powerful self to us. These religious scholars might tell us that God guided His prophets through divine intervention to shape our Bibles, Torahs or Qur'ans, so that today, we can hold God's actual words in our hands, and have a true understanding of God's greatness.

But we're here today to offer a different version of Yahweh's makeover, a different way of looking at this history. This is the story about how humans shaped God's image, not the other way around. We're going to learn how the transformation of Abraham's god-of-armies to our God Almighty is the result of an evolutionary process, the powerful and inexorable forces known as "survival of the fittest." But it was *cultural evolution*, not biological evolution, that was at work, changing and improving Yahweh's image over the millennia. And it wasn't just Yahweh who was shaped by cultural evolution; these same forces created and refined *all* of our religious beliefs.

So just what is "cultural evolution," and how does it work?

The Replicating Chicken Meme

God is a comic playing to an audience that's afraid to laugh
– Voltaire (1694-1778)

"Why did the chicken cross the road?" What a dumb joke. But you've heard it, right? And you know the retort. Why is this stupid joke one of the most pervasive and *reliable* bits of verbal information ever passed from one human to another? *Why is it passed, with extreme accuracy, to virtually every child?* What makes children tell it to each other, year after year, generation after generation?

This is not a trivial question; it illustrates a deep and profound insight into human culture, that some ideas can be passed verbally and with high fidelity, but additionally, that these facts *are* passed along whereas other ideas fade into history. Something about the chicken joke causes it to *reproduce itself.* The joke itself contains the means for its own survival – it makes children *want* to repeat it.

The chicken joke is a perfect example of a *self-replicating idea,* an idea that makes you want to repeat it to someone else. Whether it's a joke, an urban myth, a great story, or a hard lesson you've learned that you want to tell your children, each of these things carries within it the "seed" that causes it to be retold, to be copied from one human brain to another. In other words, each of these carries more than just the message itself; it also carries a *motivation* that makes you want to retell it. The message is the obvious, overt part of the joke, urban myth or lesson. The motivation is a *consequence* of the message's contents, yet it is equally important. Without the motivation, the idea would die out.

Notice that this is a lot like how our genes work: Genes carry information, just as a joke carries information. In the case of DNA, the information is chemical instructions telling a cell how to build certain proteins, a "blueprint" if you will, for the stuff your body needs to live. But the DNA's "motivation" is just as important: Those proteins ultimately cause the lifeform, whether it's a bacterium or an elephant, to copy itself, to make more copies of the DNA. Without this motivation, the DNA would die out in short order.

So your DNA shares a fascinating trait with jokes, urban myths and hard-learned lessons: They all contain a message *and* a motivation to reproduce.

Richard Dawkins was the first to recognize the parallels between ideas and genes, but he didn't think it was just an amusing analogy. Dawkins realized there was something deeper, that even though biological life and ideas are radically different, there is an important underlying theory that ties the two together. Because these self-replicating ideas were so much like genes, Dawkins coined the term *meme* (a "mnemonic gene").

A long time before Dawkins, Albert Einstein realized that energy and matter were really one and the same thing, just different aspects of a single concept. Before Einstein, the physicists Michael Faraday and James Clerk Maxwell realized that electricity and magnetism, two seemingly different phenomena, were really just two different faces of a single thing. And even earlier still, René Descartes and Pierre de Fermat showed that algebra and geometry, which might seem like two entirely different studies, were essentially the same thing, just seen from different perspectives. In each of these cases, a great mind recognized that two seemingly different ideas have a single underlying principle that, once discovered, unifies the two concepts into one and gives a deeper understanding of both.

Dawkins realized that it was the *replication of information* that was the underlying principle common to genes and ideas (memes). A century earlier, Charles Darwin had spelled out the principles of natural selection, which in spite of the staggering amount that has been written, boil down to three simple ideas: reproduction, mutation, and natural selection (survival of the fittest). If we rephrase these three ideas in information-theory terms, we would call it transcription (copying), transcription errors (mutation), and filtering (natural selection). And these concepts apply to *both* genes and memes. With this "grand unification" of the two disciplines, Dawkins laid the foundation for the study of *memetics*, which uses Darwin's evolution science to predict and explain the very foundations of human culture and knowledge.

Memes come in all flavors and sizes, but jokes are especially good examples of memes. A joke is simple, a nice little self-contained unit of information, and jokes are fun to study. They illustrate the basics of "memology" quite nicely.

The world's worst symphony conductor heard that his job was going to be given to his greatest rival. In a fit of jealousy, he murdered the rival. But,

> *being a musician, he didn't cover his tracks very*
> *well and the police immediately caught, convicted*
> *and sentenced him to death in the electric chair.*
> *When they strapped him into the chair and turned*
> *on the juice, nothing happened! He just sat there*
> *happily humming Beethoven's Ninth. They tried*
> *again and again, to no avail. Finally, he called out,*
> *"Give it up, you fools. You can't electrocute me.*
> *I'm the world's worst conductor!"*

The joke reproduced itself as you read this page, so its population just increased by one.

When I tell you a joke, I am essentially carrying out the joke's version of sex: I am using your brain to make a copy of the joke meme that was in my brain. It uses your brain's resources to keep itself alive (stored in your neurons), and if it's funny enough, you'll want to repeat the joke to someone else, thereby increasing the joke's population by one more. This sounds a lot like a virus, doesn't it?

Xeroxing Information

> *In science it often happens that scientists say, "You know*
> *that's a really good argument; my position is mistaken," and*
> *then they actually change their minds and you never hear*
> *that old view from them again. ... It happens every day. I*
> *cannot recall the last time something like that happened in*
> *politics or religion.*
> *– Carl Sagan*

Elephants are (very roughly) 1,000,000,000,000,000,000 (10^{18}) times larger than bacteria, yet they are connected by an amazing fact: Both the bacterium and the elephant contain DNA, and the ultimate goal of each elephant or bacterium is the same: *To make more copies of its DNA.* Even more amazing is that ultimately, DNA is just information. Although DNA's information is "written" as particular sequences of base pairs on the DNA strand, it's still nothing more than information, like the words on this page. Without a person to read the words on this page, it's just so many atoms. Without a living cell to interpret the gene's sequence on the DNA, it's just another chemical. A dog can't tell a page of a book from toilet paper, and a rock can't tell DNA from LSD. But with a person to read the page, or a cell to read the DNA, the information is unlocked.

And that's all a joke is: Information. But jokes, a bacterium's DNA, and an elephant's DNA have another important feature that distinguishes them from ordinary information: The very information they contain causes them to make copies of themselves. Everything else about the life of these three things is incidental to the act of copying themselves, so that their information can "live long and prosper."

Although jokes are useful to illustrate the basic idea of a meme, don't be fooled by their simplicity. Memes can be incredibly rich, complex, intertwined, and interdependent.

The Expensive Carpool Lane

> *The most savage controversies are those about matters as to which there is no good evidence either way. Persecution is used in theology, not in arithmetic*
> *— Bertrand Russell*

Here's a more modern self-replicating bit of information. While writing this book, I got the following e-mail from a relative:

```
Hi,

I just got this, pass it on.  This is serious.
Be careful you guys!

New Driving Fines for 2007
     1.  Carpool lane - 1st time $1068.50 starting
         7/1/07 (The $271 posted on the highway is
         old). Don't do it again because 2nd time
         is going to be double. 3rd time triple,
         and 4th time license suspended.
     2.  Incorrect lane change - $380. Don't cross
         the lane on solid lines or intersections.
     3.  Block intersection - $485
```

```
4.  Driving on the shoulder - $450
5.  Cell phone use in the construction zone.
    - Double fine as of 07/01/07. Cell phone
    use must be "hands free" while driving.
6.  Passengers over 18 not in their seatbelts
    - both passengers and drivers get
    tickets.
7.  Speeders can only drive 3 miles above the
    limit.
8.  DUI = JAIL (Stays on your driving record
    for 10 years!)
9.  As of 07/01/07 cell phone use must be
    "hands free" while driving. Ticket is
    $285. They will be looking for this like
    crazy - easy money for police department.
```

Sounds pretty awful, and I (like so many others) took this seriously. For a day or two, that is, until it turned up on a well-known rumor-busting web site. The whole email was a fake! All nine "new driving fines" are incorrect. Yet this email spread far and wide. Just about everyone in my own circle of family and friends received it, which means that, in a span of a few days, this "urban myth" meme went from a population of one to something like tens of millions. Wow!

This meme was perfectly crafted. It has everything that an urban myth needs:

- It is *believable*. It was carefully crafted to be slightly outrageous, but not blatantly outrageous.
- It is *relevant*. It is something we all care about. It is stuff we need to know.
- It is *scary*. We like to stir each other up.
- It is *easy to pass on*. Just click the "Forward" button on your email program, select everyone you know from your address book, and *voila!* it replicates.

Because it was so well crafted, the "New Driving Fines" urban myth became epidemic, and spread with exponential growth throughout the state.

This is a *really* good example of a meme, a self-replicating idea. It is information that, by its very nature, causes it to be copied over and over in people's minds and computers.

A Meme by Any Other Name

> *If nature has made any one thing less susceptible than all others of exclusive property, it is the action of the thinking power called an idea, which an individual may exclusively possess as long as he keeps it to himself; but the moment it is divulged, it forces itself into the possession of everyone, and the receiver cannot dispossess himself of it... He who receives an idea from me, receives instructions himself without lessening mine; as he who lights his taper at mine, receives light without darkening me. That ideas should be spread from one to another over the globe, for the moral and mutual instruction of man, and improvement of his condition, seems to have been peculiarly and benevolently designed by nature.*
> *– Thomas Jefferson (1743-1826)*

This is a remarkable quote by the brilliant statesman, scientist and philosopher, Thomas Jefferson, because it encapsulates the very idea of a meme, and predates Dawkins by nearly a century and a half.

We already learned that the definition of a meme is pretty simple: It's an idea, a concept, that is capable of being passed from one mind to another, and that produces the *motivation* that makes you want to pass it on.

Many other authors have spent varying amounts of space and intellectual energy trying to define the term, each with a slightly different skew on the subject. Is a meme strictly linguistic, or can it be a song, a painting, or the act of demonstrating how to flake obsidian to make an arrowhead? Is a meme a meme if it's stored on paper? Or in your computer? What is the difference between a *meme* and a *memeplex*? If we can't define it, how can we study it?

Careful definitions of terms are important in the erudite circles of academic philosophy, sociology, and information theory, but this is an informal book, not a scholarly tome. In my view, a meme is *any* bit of information that can be passed from one mind to another, by any mechanism. If I teach a secret handshake to a friend, and the friend thinks it's a pretty cool handshake and teaches it to you, then the secret handshake could be a meme. The key point is this: Both memes and genes are *self-replicating information*. They reproduce very differently, one via biochemical processes, and the other via person-to-person communication, but at their core, both memes and genes are just information. More importantly, *the very information contained by a gene or meme is the motivating force for its own reproduction.*

Three Sources of Knowledge

Is God willing to prevent evil, but not able? Then he is not omnipotent.
Is he able, but not willing? Then he is malevolent.
Is he both able and willing? Then whence cometh evil?
Is he neither able nor willing? Then why call him God?
– Epicurus

There are three fundamental sources of knowledge for humans: Instinct, experience, and culture.

Instinct is knowledge that is inborn. Nobody has to teach you to be afraid of heights, to go to your mother in a time of danger, to fear snakes, or that bitter foods shouldn't be eaten. Nobody has to tell a teenager to have sex (quite the contrary!). This knowledge is "hard wired" into our brains, and also into the brains of many animals.

Experience teaches you that grass feels nice under your feet, that thorns hurt if you prick your finger, and that fire is hot. *Experiential knowledge* is information that you learn by interacting with the world and the people around you. The knowledge itself isn't inborn.

Cultural learning, our highly developed ability to transmit ideas (memes) from one person to the next, is a uniquely human ability, one that makes humans truly distinct from other animals. There has been some work showing that other animals such as chimpanzees and gorillas also pass information culturally, but their abilities are primitive compared to humans.

From this, we can clearly see that our religious beliefs qualify as memes. When you were born, you didn't know anything about religion or gods (it's not instinctive knowledge), and you didn't learn about religion by interacting with nature (it's not experiential knowledge). Someone *taught* you about religion and god. Even if you don't believe in God, you still have a god meme in your head. It's a meme that was put there by your parents and community, and *they* got it from *their* parents and community, and so on down through history.

With this new memetic view that treats ideas as self-replicating pieces of information, we can now see that religion is a virus, one that infects your brain. "Right," you're probably thinking, "He means that allegorically, or metaphorically, or something. Religion is a belief system, not a germ!" But in fact, when I use the phrase *religion virus*, I mean it in a very literal sense. The religion virus isn't a physical entity, with DNA and proteins and such, but in every other sense, it is a true virus. The parallels between the viruses that infect your body and the viruses that infect your mind are truly astonishing. By the end of this book, I hope to give you a detailed understanding of the infective, reproductive, parasitic nature of the religion virus and its effect on culture, society, politics, and the future of humanity.

Our Path

> *If God did not exist, it would be necessary to invent him.* — *Voltaire (1694-1778), "Epitres, XCVI"*

We will study three paths in parallel. The first is classical Evolution Science, first elucidated by Charles Darwin, one of the greatest minds in history. Darwin's Evolution Science is astonishing in its explanatory powers; with a single book, Darwin founded what is arguably the most important science in human history. We'll just skim the surface; a full treatment requires volumes, but it's important to our story.

Second, we'll learn more about *memes*, the field of study called *memetics*. We'll learn how memes follow nearly the same evolutionary rules as the physical lifeforms that Darwin studied, as these ideas and concepts "live and reproduce" in our brains, and we'll extend Evolution Science to see how it also sheds light on cultural evolution.

And third, we'll study religion itself. We'll show that religion is explained clearly and completely by memetics and by the lessons learned from Darwin's Evolution Science. Darwin showed that God did not create Man, and now through the study of memetics, we will see that God did not even create religion. Using Darwin's principles of evolution, applied to culture via meme theory, we'll see that modern religions are the inevitable result of Darwinistic evolution of culture and ideas. In this case, survival of the fittest does not necessarily mean survival of the truest.

A Bit About Evolution

> *Surely, God could have caused birds to fly with their bones made of solid gold, with their veins full of quicksilver, with their flesh heavier than lead, and with their wings exceedingly small. He did not, and that ought to show something. It is only in order to shield your ignorance that you put the Lord at every turn to the refuge of a miracle.*
> *-- Galileo Galilei*

Most readers are familiar with Darwin's basic premise: That species evolved via a process of natural selection. Species are subject to random changes in their genome, and over millions and billions of generations, this process, which Darwin called "survival of the fittest," has given rise to the amazing diversity of plants and animals on this Earth.

We saw in the first part of this chapter that memes and genes are both examples of *self-replicating information.* It should come as no surprise, then, that the concept of "survival of the fittest" applies to memes just as it does to biological life. An idea can mutate (change) as it is passed from one person to the next; ideas compete with each other for "space" in your brain; and ideas compete for "reproduction time" by being told to the next person. The best jokes are the survivors, the worst jokes become "extinct."

As we will see, this same principle applies to religious ideas: The fittest religious ideas survive, and the unfit ones become extinct. And by "fittest" we do *not* mean the ideas that are true. Rather, these are the ideas that make people *want* to believe them, whether true or false, beneficial or harmful. An idea can be a survivor because it appeals to our hopes, our vanity, or the promise that Heaven awaits. But an idea can also be a survivor because it preys on our fears and prejudices. We're afraid of eternal punishment in Hell, we need protection from our enemies, we're afraid of dying, and we are afraid of the unknown. Ideas that prey on these fears can be just as "fit," that is, they survive just as well, as those that appeal via positive emotions.

When memes evolve, it is always towards these *survivors* – the memes that are more believable, more compelling are the ones that survive and reproduce, while the memes that are less believable and compelling fade from memory. This is the classic "survival of the fittest" rule. Keep this in mind as we begin our tour through the natural history of The Religion Virus.

Interlude: Grandpa and the Sunset

I don't know if God exists, but it would be better for His rep-
utation if He didn't.
– Jules Renard (1864-1910)

One evening when I was twelve years old, Grandpa and I stood silently on the front lawn of the huge old family farm house in the Central Valley of California, not far from Modesto. It was very quiet, the sort of quiet you only get far from the city, after the work has stopped on the farm, the tractors are silent, and the trucks on the highway have all gone on their way. A few crickets were starting their evening choir. An owl's hoot carried clearly across the forty-acre bean field from the old dairy barn on the south side, where she made her nest.

The subject that held our rapt attention was the sunset, one of those rare magnificent displays that follows a spring storm, when the air is crystal clear over the great Central Valley farmlands. The sun's fading rays illuminated the underside of the high, lingering clouds, making them glow in all colors, from bright orange near the horizon, to brilliant red above us, to a dull purple behind us against the faint outline of the snow-capped Sierra Nevada mountains, all set against a sky so blue and clear it made you dizzy.

As the sunset faded, Grandpa said without turning, "I don't know how you can witness such magnificence and not believe in God."

Without thinking, the twelve-year-old version of me replied, "I don't see the connection, Grandpa. Einstein explained why the sky is blue and the sunset's red. He got a Nobel Prize for it. It's because of the photoelectric effect. You see, the oxygen..."

Grandpa turned and looked at me, and I stopped. Grandpa was an unusual man, a farmer with a degree from the University of California. In fact, my Grandfather was in the very first class at UC Davis in 1929, where I also got my bachelor's degree forty-nine years later. Grandpa knew about science, and a bit about physics, and Grandpa knew I was a science nerd.

There was a moment's silence. "I don't know how I'd survive without God, son. My life has been very hard and full of misery, but I've kept going because I know I'll get my reward when I die. And every now and then, God shows me His glory in a sunset."

I didn't know what to say. Grandpa's life miserable? How could this be?

"Even if you don't believe in God, son, you should take time whenever you can to stop and watch His glorious sunsets. Never forget that."

And I never did. I still think of Grandpa whenever I see a sunset. I know Einstein explained it in 1906, but it's still one of the most beautiful things I've ever seen. Thanks, Grandpa.

But I'll also never forget those sad words, "I don't know how I'd survive without God." Those eight words were a prison for my Grandpa. He used an imaginary reward in heaven to help him accept his misery. Instead of making his life better, he did what men and women have been taught to do for thousands of years: Accept your fate, don't complain, *don't question your life, because your reward comes later.*

Grandpa taught me more with those eight sad words than anything he could have explained about God's majesty revealed in a sunset. His resignation inspired me to make my life better, to fix the things that are wrong in my life, and to *never give up the fight.* There is no heaven, and there is no hell. If my life sucks now, I have to make it better *now*, because there is no second chance.

And my life is good. Thanks for that lesson, too, Grandpa.

2. Religion's Infancy

The modern-day Western "Abrahamic" religions (Judaism, Christianity and Islam) are all woven from a common fabric. We begin our study of the Religion Virus with eight major ideas that developed in the millennia leading up to the birth of Jesus. As we study each idea, try to think of it as a meme – an evolving, reproducing entity that is competing with other memes, trying to survive, trying to get passed on to the next generation, just like a gene. Most studies of religious history focus on *how* various ideas gained importance and were incorporated into each religion. In our version of history, we will learn *why* these ideas survived, while so many others did not.

The General-Purpose God Meme

If God were suddenly condemned to live the life which He has inflicted upon men, He would kill Himself.
– Alexandre Dumas, fils

The island of New Guinea is just north of Australia at the southwest edge of the Pacific Ocean, and is the world's second-largest island. It was "discovered" by Europeans in the early 16th century, but largely ignored until the mid-1800s, when missionaries and traders began to settle there. New Guinea was variously claimed and abandoned by a string of European nations; eventually the Western half, Irian Jaya (now called Papua), became a territory of Indonesia, and in 1975 the Eastern part gained independence and is today called Papua New Guinea.

In the 1930s, something remarkable happened. New Guinea's interior is very steep mountainous, carpeted by thick rain forests, and it was believed to be completely uninhabited. The Dutch government, hoping for profits from their colony, mounted an expedition into the interior, looking for gold or other minerals in the rugged mountains. Much to their surprise, instead of an uninhabited jungle, they found a civilization. And not just a few sparse settlements, but *almost a million people.* Over the next few decades, the ongoing discoveries of more and more of the tribes in these impossibly steep and rugged highlands was electrifying news to the anthropology community; it was actually the last great discovery of a large, "primitive" society in the history of the world. In spite of the technological miracles of the twentieth century, a million people were still almost completely isolated from the rest of humanity.

One of these New Guinean highlands tribes is called the *Amung.* Due to the steep mountains and deep valleys of the New Guinean highlands, the highland peoples were mostly isolated from the lowlanders, and many of the tribes were even isolated from each other for thousands of years. Before they were relocated by the Dutch Government and priests of the Catholic Church to make way for exploitation of their land, the Amung occupied seventeen valleys in the Sudirman Mountains.

The Amung had a typical animism spiritual belief system, where "anima" is used in its root form to mean "animated," or literally, the *soul.* Dr. Carolyn D. Turinsky Cook studied the Amung extensively; she writes:

> *Indigenous peoples like the Amung, believe that all matter is fundamentally alive. Life can be found in rocks, trees, mountains and rivers as well as in people. ... Their belief system contains a combination of earth spirits [and] ancestor spirits ...*

In other words, the Amung did not have an idea of "gods" that are separate from nature; spirits and nature were one and the same. Their religion wasn't separate from their lives, such as a church that you attend only on Sunday; instead, they were immersed in their religion throughout their lives. In a sense, the spirits are part of the community rather than separate from it.

If you counted gods down through the centuries since recorded history began, there would be one glaring trend: As the centuries go by, there are fewer and fewer gods, but those that remain are vested with more and more powers.

The earliest beliefs that can be identified as religious are usually *animism*, like the Amung people's society. That is, people would "animate" the objects that were important to their survival. Crops and trees, deer and bears, the sun and moon, rainclouds, a spear or axe – all of the things that were important to people – were imagined to have personalities and motivations. A tricky whirlpool in the river wants to suck the canoe to doom, and the canoeist must outwit it (it's personal, the canoeist versus the whirlpool). A cloud may have sympathy for a village and provide rain if the village pleads their need and performs the correct ritual. A deer may agree to sacrifice itself if the hunter explains that his children are hungry.

These spirits must be variously consulted, avoided, appeased, tricked, and prayed to, as part of everyday life. People in these societies interact with these spirits much like they interact with each other – as more-or-less equals. Each spirit has an obvious and direct purpose: The deer's spirit protects the deer, the moon's spirit guides it across the sky, and the cloud's spirit decides when rain should fall. If you need the spirit's help, you ask for it.

Dr. Turinsky Cook writes about the Amung people's daily lives:

No place of any significance, even the smallest, the rocks, the hills, and streams ever went without a name in the Amung land. The Amung mountains to the north are the domain of their ancestor spirits. They are sacred and connected to many myths and legends. Daily life reflects the place of spirituality and the connection of the Amung to their land. ...

The values and regulations in the Amung social system reveal a respect and fear of some power other than that of people, be it ancestor spirits [or] earth spirits... This gives them a basic framework for their interactions with other people.

As time passes and societies mature, "meta spirits" (literally, spirits above the spirits) arise that are tied to groups rather than specific objects: There might be a bear spirit in charge of all bear-individuals, or a weather spirit in charge of all clouds. These spirits become more powerful with time, and have less and less attachment to the physical world. The borderline between "spirit" and "god" is a grey area, but after a while, these spirits become more and more powerful, and are properly called gods.

Once gods become abstract (not tied to a specific object), the next development is gods for *concepts* rather than *things*. These gods can answer prayers for *abstract* concepts, such as love, justice, and war. Praying to the spirit of a rock or deer doesn't help a jilted lover, but praying to a god might.

This was the first step in the evolution of the *General Purpose God* meme. Religion had evolved from animism gods (spirits) that were tied to specific, physical things (a bear, a tree) with a narrowly defined purpose, to gods that were responsible for whole classes of things (all bears, all trees), and then to things that are purely conceptual (love) or were human activities (war).

The trend of fewer, more powerful gods continues: The gods begin taking on multiple tasks, so that you might pray to one god for several things. The diminishing set of gods also takes on a hierarchy, with greater and lesser gods. Sooner or later a greatest god emerges, sometimes a mother figure, sometimes a father figure.

This trend in the history of religious development spans an amazing array of human societies. Certainly not all societies, and certainly there are societies which haven't reached the "endpoint" of monotheism, but in broad terms, societies tend to start with animism, then move to a polytheistic religion, and then towards a hierarchy of gods, which culminates in a few a few dominant gods or a single god. This is a sweeping generalization, but it gives us an important overall picture.

Neither Abraham (about 2000 to 1900 BCE), nor Moses (around 1200 BCE) were monotheists. They were immersed in and part of a polytheistic culture that included many gods. Abraham and his descendants, down to Moses and the Israelites, did *not* believe that Yahweh (today's "God") was the only god. They believed in, and sometimes worshipped, the gods Baal, Asherah, Anat, and many others.

According to the Book of Genesis, Abraham made a covenant with God ("El"), promising that in exchange for sole recognition of El as his supreme deity, Abraham would be blessed with innumerable progeny, and God would protect and favor Abraham's people. Clearly Abraham was a pagan: Why would El ask for loyalty if Abraham was already a monotheist? When Abraham agreed to this covenant, Yahweh (who wasn't called by that name yet) became the Israelites' protector, and the Israelites promised to forgo worshipping the other gods.

But this didn't work very well. How could one pray to Yahweh, a war god, for fertility or good crops? Most of the Israelites knew this. They paid their homage to Yahweh, but they also prayed to the traditional gods as the need arose. The Israelites thought it would be foolhardy to ignore the blessings that other gods could provide, just because Yahweh was jealous. In times of peace, it was easy to forget the covenant that Abraham made with God.

By the time of Moses, plenty of war, plague and pestilence had been rained down on the Israelites, and the traditionalists claimed that this was their punishment: They were ignoring Abraham's covenant with El, and they'd lost the favor of God. So according to the Biblical history, Yahweh appeared before Moses, and essentially started over: A new covenant was made, Yahweh issued new laws, and the Israelites renewed their commitment to worship only Yahweh.

It is especially interesting to note that when Yahweh appears to Moses in the burning bush, he insists that he is in fact El Shaddai, the god of Abraham.

I am the God of your father, the God of Abraham, the God
of Isaac, and the God of Jacob.
– Exodus 3:6

Moses believed in many gods, so Yahweh had to explain to Moses exactly which god Moses was talking to; that not only was He the God of Moses' own father, he was *also* the God of Abraham and his descendants. Indeed, Yahweh emphasizes four times in Exodus 3 that He is the same god that Abraham worshipped.

Now the Israelites were really in a bind. They'd promised their loyalty to Yahweh twice, first with Abraham, and again with Moses. Yet Yahweh's command prohibiting the worship of other gods was problematic: How could Yahweh, who was also known as Yahweh Sabaoth, the God of Armies, help when it came to delivering a healthy baby, or ensuring a good harvest? To whom should a young maiden pray to for love? To whom could the sick father pray to get his health back so that he could once again care for his family? Who would answer a prayer for a sick bull to get well? This introduced a strain into the religion of the Israelites: Their promise to Yahweh was at odds with their spiritual needs.

As time went by, the Israelites' concept of Yahweh followed the path we described above: Yahweh became (in their minds) more and more powerful, finally becoming the master of all things, not just war. It was said that Yahweh could answer all prayers, and more and more Israelites found it acceptable to pray only to Yahweh. By the time of Jesus, the Jews believed Yahweh was the "almighty," creator of the universe, all-wise and all-knowing, and *able to answer all prayers*.

This was the final step in the evolution of the *General-Purpose-God* meme. Previously, Yahweh could demand absolute loyalty from the Israelites, but it was hard for them to obey because they needed other gods' help. But after the Yahweh meme evolved to be a general-purpose god, for the first time in human history it became possible for a god to demand, *and receive*, absolute loyalty.

Why was the General-Purpose God meme a good mutation for the Yahweh memeplex? Because a "one stop shopping" god meme is easier to worship than a bunch of specialty god-memes. You can make all your requests in a single prayer. The Yahweh meme had transitioned from a specialty god who could only serve you in war, to a god who served your every need. This was a huge step toward making Yahweh into the Almighty God we know today.

While this story may be new to some readers, any historian would point out that we've just retold a story that can be found in thousands of history books, including the Old Testament itself. This is where our study of memes comes in. History books tell us *what* happened, but Darwin's principles of evolution, applied to memes, can help us understand *why* it happened.

The General-Purpose-God meme, at each point in history, was not a single concept, but rather was a large body of similar ideas being taught by parents, teachers and religious leaders to each other and to the next generation of children. The General-Purpose-God meme essentially tells us, "Which prayers can Yahweh answer?"

You can think of each person's particular answer to this question an "individual meme", and the whole society's group of answers as a "species of memes" that is evolving. Like plants and animals, each individual (each person's specific answer to the question, "Which prayers can Yahweh answer?") has some probability of reproducing, of somebody else accepting that answer into his/her own set of beliefs. "Survival of the fittest" means that the more likable, appealing versions of the Yahweh will spread, and the dislikable versions will lose popularity and become extinct. This process continued with each generation. Ideas are not static, but constantly shift as they are retold, as society changes, as the physical environment (the world) changes, and as many other forces change people's ideas. As the generations and millennia passed, the *All-Purpose God* meme continued to vary, to be retold in different ways, and different versions were believed to varying degrees by the next generation.

By the time of Jesus, the answer to this question, "Which prayers can Yahweh answer?" was radically different than in Abraham's time. Abraham's god-of-armies Yahweh was a specialist, a god of war; the *All-Purpose God* meme hadn't evolved yet. But the relentless process of mutation and selection altered this aspect of Yahweh. The *All-Purpose God* meme was the survivor, while the god-of-war meme became extinct.

The Monotheism Meme

The gods too are fond of a joke.
– Aristotle (384-322 BC)

When Yahweh became an all-purpose god, it was no longer necessary to worship other gods – Yahweh could handle all the prayer needs of the Israelites. But this did *not* make the Jews monotheists, far from it. Although they only worshipped Yahweh, many or most Israelites were pagans for the centuries leading up to the time of Moses. The idea that Yahweh was the only god would have seemed absurd to most Israelites, even though they worshipped Yahweh exclusively.

In Abraham's time, the Israelites, and pretty much everyone in the world, were polytheists, and actively worshipped many gods. According to the Abrahamic history known as the Tanakh (Jews) or the Old Testament (Christians), God ("El") revealed himself to Abraham. Although the seed of monotheism was started, it didn't really take hold until the time of Moses, and even then, the Jews weren't completely converted to monotheism until around the time of Jesus. Old traditions die hard. Most Israelites knew that Yahweh was their special god, but they also believed in the traditional gods.

We can see this in a number of biblical passages, for example:

Now I know that the LORD is greater than all gods: for in
the thing wherein they dealt proudly he was above them.
– Exodus 18:11

The temple I am going to build will be great, because our
God is greater than all other gods.
– 2 Chronicles 2:5

The rise of true monotheism among the Jews took hold with Moses, a story that we outlined briefly in the previous section, the *General-Purpose God* meme. During Moses' time, the Jews renewed their covenant with Yahweh, but more importantly, over the next millennium, they slowly became convinced that Yahweh was the only god, and that the other gods were fictional. Strictly speaking, Moses' people were *henotheistic,* that is, they were devoted to one god, Yahweh, but believed in the existence of many gods.

By the time the prophet Isaiah had his revelation (ca 746 BCE), monotheism was getting a strong foothold in Jewish theology:

> *Remember the former things of old: for I am God, and there is none else; I am God, and there is none like me,*
> *– Isaiah 44:9*

And shortly after Isaiah, Deuteronomy had a profound influence on the rise of monotheism among the Jews. Although the authorship and date of Deuteronomy is uncertain, it seems to have been written around 700 BCE. Deuteronomy contains at least a dozen warnings against idolatry, which is clearly seen as a rebellion against Yahweh. In Deuteronomy, there is no room for polytheism.

But polytheism was not dead yet among the Jews – many still worshipped the old gods. The prophet Jeremiah, who lived at the time of the destruction of Solomon's Temple (around 587/6 BC), had to listen to the complaints of the Jewish women of Egypt:

> *"We will not listen to your messages from the Lord! We will do whatever we want. We will burn incense and pour out liquid offerings to the Queen of Heaven [Isis/Ishtar] just as much as we like – just as we, and our ancestors, and our kings and officials have always done in the towns of Judah and in the streets of Jerusalem. For in those days we had plenty to eat, and we were well off and had no troubles! But ever since we quit burning incense to the Queen of Heaven and stopped worshiping her with liquid offerings, we have been in great trouble and have been dying from war and famine."*
> *– Jeremiah 44:15-18*

In spite of incidents like this one, the Jewish people were becoming more and more monotheistic. Jewish rabbis and philosophers argued that Yahweh was not only their special god, but that he was the *only* god. Yahweh morphed from a god with whom Abraham dined with as one might a neighbor, to a mighty god that Moses addressed in person but with great fear, to an almighty, all-knowing, and also unknowable, and *unique* supreme being.

The *Monotheism* meme has had a profound influence on its believers, convincing them that not only is Yahweh the one god, but also erasing and revising their own history, convincing believers of the meme that the Israelites were always monotheists. Yet polytheism can be plainly seen in the Old Testament where it discusses the other gods:

> *God standeth in the congregation of the mighty; he judgeth among the gods. ... I have said, Ye are gods; and all of you are children of the most High. But ye shall die like men, and fall like one of the princes.*
> *– Psalm 82*

> *Who is like unto thee, O Lord, among the gods?*
> *– Exodus 15:11*

> *And the king will do according to his pleasure; and he will exalt himself and magnify himself over every god, and against the God of gods he will speak outrageous things...*
> *– Daniel 11:35*

> *For thou, Lord, art high above all the earth: thou art exalted far above all gods.*
> *– Psalm 97:9*

The *Monotheism* meme has been so effective that today, most Jews, Christians and Muslims don't even realize that the Israelites from Abraham's time down to Moses' time were polytheists. The *Monotheism* meme has wiped out the genuine polytheistic history, and replaced it with a history in which the Jews were monotheistic from the start.

What can Darwin's theory of evolution tell us about monotheism? One of the most interesting outcomes of natural selection and "survival of the fittest" is that if any two species fill the same ecological niche, that is, if both "make their living" the exact same way, one will quickly dominate and the other will become extinct. Two species that are in perfect balance in the same ecological niche are like a pin balanced on its point: It's an inherently unstable situation, and the pin will fall one way or the other no matter how perfectly you balance it. In the case of competing species, if one has even the slightest survival advantage over the other (and in real life, there are always differences), the relentless forces of natural selection make quick work of the less-adapted species.

In primitive animism, each spirit has a very specific ecological niche – the bear spirit does bear stuff, and the cloud spirit does weather stuff, and the two don't compete at all for survival. They "live" in separate ecological niches. But, we already learned how, as time passed, the multitude of spirits narrowed down into fewer gods, and then into just a few gods. At the same time, these gods become more general, and therein lies the problem: At some point, their "ecological niches" started to overlap, and they started competing with one another for attention. Just as in nature, if two gods serve the same purpose, it's unlikely that both will survive.

There is a remarkable parallel between Yahweh's evolution and humankind's. Humans have become generalists: We can live almost anywhere on Earth, and can eat just about anything. We have become competitors to just about every large animal on Earth, and in fact many species have been pushed to the brink of extinction, or are actually extinct, because we humans have encroached on their resources, taken over or destroyed their habitat, or consumed all their food or water.

In just the same way, Yahweh became a generalist. He usurped the roles of all other gods, causing the extinction of nearly all of them in the Western world. Memetic evolution theory predicts exactly what we find in today's religions: The many gods of earlier times have been replaced by a generalist, a single god that has taken over the "religion ecosphere."

The Intolerance Meme

In every country and in every age, the priest has been hostile to liberty. He is always in alliance with the despot, abetting his abuses in return for protection to his own.
– Thomas Jefferson, Letter to H. Spafford, 1814

Old gods, including Yahweh, had flaws that were remarkably human in nature. Dionysus (also known as Bacchus) was the god of wine, party and fertility. Apollo killed Marsyas for besting him in a music contest. Aphrodite is almost always characterized as unfaithful to her husband, vain, bad-tempered and easy to offend. The "sins" of Zeus are almost too many to count: Rapist, murderer, pederast, liar, and torturer. Queen Isis, though worshipped as the perfect wife and mother, was incestuously married to her brother. And Yahweh himself is well documented for the floods, plagues and other calamities he caused.

But for all of their flaws, the Greek and Roman gods, and in fact the gods of all pagan religions, had one universal virtue: They didn't require their worshippers to *kill* anyone who worshipped another god. That distinction belongs to Yahweh.

In ancient times, no matter which god you worshipped at home, it was considered good manners, and a good idea, to pay respects to the god of your host when you visited. Travelers would, as a matter of politeness, stop into the local temples and make offerings to the local gods, and the gods of their hosts. It was also common, indeed required, to worship different gods for different purposes. There was no point worshipping a love goddess when you were planting your crops, or making an offering to a war god when you were hoping for better weather. For most of humanity's history, the idea of worshipping just one god was unthinkable.

The corollary to this is that pagan worshippers are not usually inclined to tell one another how or whom to worship. Polytheism is inherently a tolerant set of beliefs, a sort of live-and-let-live philosophy. To the pagan, the choice of which god to worship is pragmatic and situational, that is, it depends on what you need and why you are praying. A man or woman who worshipped the "wrong" god might be considered foolish, but it was hardly an affront to other worshippers.

Certainly there were exceptions. The best known resulted in the Maccabeen Revolt, which is celebrated as Hanukkah by the Jews. Antiochus Epiphanes, emperor of the Seleucid Empire, had prohibited Jewish religious practices, defiled the Second Temple of Jerusalem, and demanded that the Jews pay homage to the Greek gods. Mattathias the Hasmonean and his five sons (known as the Maccabees) sparked a revolt that ultimately overthrew the Syrian rule and restored the Second Temple and the Jew's religious freedom.

However, even this example of pagan religious intolerance is not what it seems. In fact, it was not a religious intolerance at all; rather, it was a strategic battle tactic: The anti-Jewish edicts issued by Antiochus were simply a way of flushing out his enemies. By the time of Antiochus, most Jews were monotheists, and were remarkable (for that time) in that they refused, even under pain of death, to worship other gods, to work on the Sabbath, or to eat pork. Antiochus recognized this for what it was: a military vulnerability. Jews could easily be identified, especially the hard-line Jews, by asking them to pay respects to a god besides Yahweh.

Ironically, even though the Jews were victims of persecution for their religion, it was the Jewish religion that became the cradle of religious intolerance.

Prior to Antiochus' anti-Jewish edicts and the Maccabee revolt, the Jews had already laid the three cornerstones of the foundation of religious intolerance. We've already studied them: The *General-Purpose-God* meme, the *Monotheism* meme, and Moses' covenant with Yahweh to make Yahweh the *exclusive god of the Jews*. In a nutshell, these three ideas taught that you *could* worship just one god, you *should* worship just one god, and that *all other gods are false*. That is, the Jews invented the idea that, "We are right, and you are wrong."

The real birth of the *Intolerance* meme is described in the book of Deuteronomy, probably written around 700 BCE, when it became *forbidden* and *sinful* to worship other gods. Prior to that, even though the Jews believed that they were Yahweh's chosen people, and that Yahweh's protection depended on their fidelity to Yahweh, the Jews had no real issue with those who didn't follow their faith. Like the pagans, the Jews simply considered others misguided. But with Deuteronomy, the *Intolerance* meme had finally matured; now worship of other gods was considered a mortal affront to Yahweh, and had to be suppressed.

The genesis of the *Intolerance* meme triggered one of the of the first great acts of religious genocide, by the Jewish king Josiah (622 BCE):

> *In his twelfth year he began to purge Judah and Jerusalem of high places, Asherah poles, carved idols and cast images. Under his direction the altars of the Baals were torn down; he cut to pieces the incense altars that were above them, and smashed the Asherah poles, the idols and the images. ... He burned the bones of the priests on their altars ... he tore down the altars and the Asherah poles and crushed the idols to powder and cut to pieces all the incense altars throughout Israel.*
> *– 2 Chronicles 34*

It was a terrible tragedy in the history of humankind. But it was justified by the newly evolved *Intolerance* meme:

and when the LORD your God has delivered them over to you and you have defeated them, then you must destroy them totally. Make no treaty with them, and show them no mercy. ... Break down their altars, smash their sacred stones, cut down their Asherah poles and burn their idols in the fire. ... The LORD your God has chosen you out of all the peoples on the face of the earth to be his people, his treasured possession. ... You must destroy all the peoples the LORD your God gives over to you. Do not look on them with pity and do not serve their gods, for that will be a snare to you
– from Deuteronomy 7

This was a very important mutation in the religion memeplexes. For the first time, a major religion had an official, written policy that other religion memeplexes were to be *actively destroyed*, rather than ignored or tolerated.

Compare this to biological evolution. The Yahweh memeplex reinvented one of the strategies we find in the animal kingdom: In addition to out-breeding competitors, you can also *kill* your competitors outright to make room for your own offspring. An unpleasant example of this is found in primate species such as chimpanzees. Dr. Jane Goodall reported that a male chimpanzee will sometimes murder the infant child of an unfamiliar female. While this horrifies us, it makes evolutionary sense: Chimpanzees are promiscuous within their own group, so a male chimpanzee can't know which infants in his group are his own offspring. But the infant of a female who has recently joined the group is certainly not the child of any male in the group. By murdering the infant, the male chimpanzee makes the female come into fertility sooner, which increases his own chances of fathering a child by her.

This is exactly what the Yahweh memeplex did, as chronicled in Deuteronomy: Rather than competing with the other god memes on merit (Which god can grant the most prayers? Which god can protect his worshippers best?), the Yahweh meme mutated, causing its believers to *kill* the believers of other god memes. By destroying the other religion's temples and murdering their priests, the Yahweh meme increased its own chances of survival and reproduction, just as the chimpanzee male did by murdering the unfamiliar infant.

The Globalization Meme

Religion is a man using a divining rod. Philosophy is a man using a pick and shovel.
– Author Unknown

We've already discussed how the earliest religions, which were mostly *animism*, put spirits in various objects, such as animals and trees. At the other end of history, we find that Yahweh, God of the Jews, Muslims and Christians, created the universe, pervades everything, and knows everything. That's quite a change in how supernatural beings are viewed.

When first conceived, a god or supernatural being is usually tied to a particular place.

At one time they lived in Mesopotamia, because they [the Israelites] did not wish to follow the gods of their ancestors who were in Chaldea. Since they had abandoned the ways of their ancestors, and worshiped the God of heaven, the God they had come to know, their ancestors drove them out from the presence of their gods.
– Book of Judith, 5:7-8

In other words, the old gods of the Israelites' ancestors were *local* gods, tied to a particular region. If you left that region, your gods couldn't hear your prayers.

A god's meme can mutate via the *Globalization* meme, that is, the god breaks loose from that place and becomes a god of a wider area, or of the whole world. Once globalized, the god can answer prayers, help friends, and punish enemies, anywhere in the world.

Imagine that Hawai'ian worshippers decided to spread a cult of Pele, Goddess of the Volcano, to the rest of the world. To begin with, Pele lives on Mauna Loa, and is well known for her violent temper, and for giving out justice. Those who are cruel or disrespectful have their homes or crops destroyed by the lava from her volcano. But if the Hawai'ians sent a missionary to the Dine'é (Navajo Nation) of America's southwest, they would be unlikely to get any converts. The Diné would probably respect the Hawai'ian's god, but it would be a waste of time for the Diné to worship Pele – what good could it possibly bring? How could Pele punish the Diné who were cruel or disrespectful? Pele lives on Mauna Loa, and her lava can't reach the Diné.

Even Yahweh started out as a regional god. During the time of Exodus, when the Jews had to leave their homeland, many feared that they would be in foreign lands where Yahweh could no longer hear them. This fear seems silly today, but only because the *Globalization* meme has done its work: All Abrahamic religions now believe that Yahweh is a universal god, who can be worshipped from anywhere. And, like the *Monotheism* meme, the *Globalization* meme has altered history, such that most who worship Yahweh today would deny that their ancestors thought of Yahweh as anything but the Almighty God. But it wasn't trivial at the time of Exodus, because the *Globalization* meme hadn't done its full work yet; leaving their homeland and their god was a huge blow to some of the Israelites.

One of the most brilliant insights of Charles Darwin was his argument that population size alone is a predictor of the survival of a species. Let's imagine there are two species of wolves that compete with each other for food, shelter and other resources, and that one of the two species has a much larger range, and many more individual wolves, than the other. All else being equal, the larger population of wolves is *much* more likely to survive and supplant the smaller population than the other way around. Why is this?

To begin with, the more populous wolf species is more likely to survive a catastrophe (a bitter winter, a deadly disease) just because there are more of them. But more importantly, the larger population of wolves has more genetic diversity, and variations ("mutations") of the genes are the raw material for evolution. As conditions change, new competitors arrive, new diseases attack, and so forth, the larger population's greater genetic diversity makes it more likely that it will be able to adapt. "Survival of the fittest" only works when there are differences between individuals, and the larger population has more differences.

Going back to the *Globalization* meme, which converted Yahweh from a regional god to a god who could be worshipped any-where, we can now see why this is important. A regional god-meme has a small population, and less diversity (fewer "mutations") than a god who is worshipped over a wide area. As Yahweh's territory expanded, the Yahweh meme became more and more likely to sur-vive. Like the wolves, no single catastrophe (a religious massacre, a competing religion) was likely to destroy it, and like any large popu-lation, the increased diversity in the species (that is, various notions of who/what Yahweh is) provided better adaptability, more "raw material" for the process of natural selection to work on.

Without the *Globalization* meme, Judaism, Christianity, and Islam would be nothing more than a local phenomenon in the Middle East, and might have died out altogether. But with it, these three religions have spread widely.

The Abstract-God Meme

Religion is a monumental chapter in the history of human egotism.
– William James

The gods of primitive societies usually aren't much different from humans. In fact, they were thought to be "of the Earth," that is, made of the same stuff as you and me, only vested with supernatural powers. In fact, many early gods are thought to originate as ordinary humans, but upon their death, they gain godly powers.

The Hawai'ian goddess Pele, mentioned in the previous section, is an example of such a god. According to legend, Pele was a Tahi-tian girl with a violent temper who, because of constant fighting (in particular with her sister), was exiled from Tahiti. She set off in a canoe, pursued by her sister; the two eventually fought near Hana on the island of Maui, where Pele was torn apart by her sister. She became a goddess at that point, and made her home in the volcano Kilauea on Mauna Loa, on the Big Island of Hawai'i.

Pele was what we might call a same-stuff-as-us god: She was made of earthly matter, even though she had supernatural powers.

The Yahweh of Abraham and Moses was also a same-stuff-as-us god. Consider these passages:

> *So Jacob was left alone, and a man wrestled with him till daybreak. When the man saw that he could not overpower him, he touched the socket of Jacob's hip so that his hip was wrenched as he wrestled with the man. Then the man said, "Let me go, for it is daybreak." But Jacob replied, "I will not let you go unless you bless me." The man asked him, "What is your name?" "Jacob," he answered. Then the man said, "Your name will no longer be Jacob, but Israel, because you have struggled with God and with men and have overcome.*
> *– Genesis 32*

By the first century BCE, this sort of story would have been absurd to the Jews – that a man could wrestle Yahweh to a draw. But when Genesis was written, it made perfect sense, because Yahweh was a same-stuff-as-humans god. And consider this:

> *The LORD appeared to Abraham near the great trees of Mamre while he was sitting at the entrance to his tent in the heat of the day. Abraham looked up and saw three men standing nearby.*
> *– Genesis 18:1*

Abraham seems to know right away that this is Yahweh and two angels, because he immediately offers them hospitality. But Abraham's wife Sarah laughs at Yahweh's prediction that Sarah, who was already very old, would have a child. It's only when Yahweh says, "Is anything too hard for the Lord?" that Sarah suddenly realizes who this man is, and becomes frightened because she laughed at His prediction.

Many generations later, the Yahweh of Moses has become more exalted, yet he still visits Moses in person in Moses' tent. Moses request to see Yahweh's glory, but Yahweh explains that,

> *"I will cause all my goodness to pass in front of you, and I will proclaim my name, the LORD, in your presence. ... But," he said, "you cannot see my face, for no one may see me and live. ... There is a place near me where you may stand on a rock. When my glory passes by, I will put you in a cleft in the rock and cover you with my hand until I have passed by. Then I will remove my hand and you will see my back; but my face must not be seen."*
> *– Exodus 33:19-23*

In other words, Yahweh was still an of-this-Earth god, made of the same stuff as you and me, but his exaltedness and powers had increased such that no mortal man could look on his face, only his back.

A "same stuff as us" god, such as Abraham's or Moses' Yahweh, is hard to reconcile with the idea that "God created the universe." We've already studied three other related memes: *General-Purpose God* (answers all prayers); *Monotheism* (the one and only god); and *Globalization* (god is everywhere). How could a god who fit these three criteria also be made of the same stuff as you and me? How could a god who created the universe also be *part* of the universe?

This question didn't trouble the Israelites very much until well after the time of Moses, possibly because the above-mentioned three memes weren't fully developed yet. Yahweh had changed quite a lot from Abraham's time, becoming more powerful and much less like an ordinary human, yet the Israelites had not really formulated the question, "Is Yahweh of this world, or separate from it?" Yahweh was powerful, but was still a god who occupied the same world as humans.

In another part of the world, the Greeks were developing one of the most influential schools of philosophy in the history of the world. Beginning with Thales, Pythagoras and the other pre-Socratic philosophers, the Greeks started to reject mystical explanations of nature and look for *rational* explanations. We must be careful here when using the word "rational," because it might seem to imply that other religions were "irrational" in the modern, negative sense of that word, which is *not* what we mean. The word "rational," when used to describe philosophy, has a very specific, mathematical-like definition. It means a system of beliefs in which truth is not found in sensory or emotional evidence, but rather starts from known truths, then uses intellect and deductive logic to extend the truth to new areas. This study of rational thought continued through Socrates, Plato and Aristotle, names that even today are known to virtually everyone in the Western world.

The Greeks, particularly Aristotle, gave a great deal of thought to the origins of the universe, and were the first to formulate a clear question about body-versus-soul and a material-versus-ethereal god. That is, is the human soul made of the same stuff as the human body, and are gods made of the same stuff as the universe?

In Aristotle's theology, the creator could not be a personal god, and could not logically be both the creator of the world, and be part of that world, for how could a god be part of the world that he himself had created? Using the methods of rational thought, Aristotle concluded that, once the universe was created, the creator could not influence it or be influenced by it. Because of this separation, he coined the term "Unmoved Mover" to capture his concept of the creator.

The Jews and Greeks were thrown together by history in the fourth century BCE, when Alexander of Macedonia defeated Darius III of Persia, and the Greeks began to move eastward into Asia and on to Africa. The Jews encountered a culture steeped in Greek Rationalism, and a culture that had no acquaintance with their god, Yahweh. As with many invasions, the two cultures began mixing, each learning from and contributing to the other. Many Jews found Greek rationalism exciting and innovative. The Greeks were still strongly polytheistic, so it was easy for them to include a study of Yahweh in their religion. The Greeks read the Jewish scriptures (which were quickly translated to Greek, producing the version known as the Septuagint), and often listened to the sermons of the Jewish rabbis.

Aristotle's Unmoved Mover was intellectually interesting, but was a distant, impersonal god. Compared to the Yahweh that the Jews worshipped, Aristotle's Unmoved Mover was boring. (From our memetic point of view, Aristotle's Unmoved Mover was not a *survivor* meme – it didn't appeal to the masses and so became extinct.) Yet, the Greek Rationalists' philosophy had a strong influence on the Jews, because it raised the question: Is Yahweh the same stuff as the world, or is Yahweh something different?

The intellectual peace between the Greeks and Jews didn't last long – the Jews' monotheism and refusal to honor Greek gods was offensive to the Greeks. But the seed was sown, the questions asked.

In parallel with the Greek rationalist "invasion" into Jewish thought, the Jews' concept of Yahweh was getting more and more exalted and abstract, under the influence of the *General-Purpose God*, *Monotheism*, and *Globalization* memes. This abstraction became problematic: How could such an exalted Yahweh sit down to dinner with Abraham, or have any of the numerous conversations described in the Torah?

This caused a dissonance in the Jewish beliefs. On the one hand, the Torah had a number of stories that described Yahweh in plain terms as though he was a same-stuff-as-us god. On the other hand, the Greeks had introduced Rationalism that couldn't be ignored, showing that such a god was logically impossible. Jewish scholars debated this question, and introduced various explanations of these stories, and of Yahweh. Recall that polytheism was not entirely gone from Jewish culture in the time between Moses and Jesus, so some believed that Yahweh was created by a greater god. Others argued that the rationalists were wrong, that a god such as Yahweh wasn't bound by logic and could both create the universe and be part of it. And others argued for a Yahweh more like Aristotle's, one who was separate from the universe; that the stories of Yahweh were metaphorical, not historical.

In the end, the meme that survived, the "fittest," was a new blend of ideas, one that could satisfy both the Rationalists and the historical accounts in Genesis. The new meme said that Yahweh was separated from his actions on Earth. This new concept states that we can never know Yahweh himself, who is utterly beyond human comprehension, but Yahweh is able to alter events on Earth, or speak to humans, by creating apparitions (using earthly matter) that serve his purpose on Earth. It was these apparitions, not Yahweh himself, that Jacob wrestled with, and with whom Moses made his covenant.

This is the real genesis of the *Abstract God* meme. God is not the same-stuff-as-us, but rather is a different, unknowable being, outside of the material universe, which He created, yet he can still act in the material world by making physical apparitions that we simple humans can tolerate and comprehend.

Notice how the Jews' new concept of Yahweh was an improvement on both their own theology, and on Aristotle's. Aristotle's Unmoved Mover failed the test of evolutionary survivability, because there was nothing to worship. Why pray to a god who can't interact with your universe? The Jews had adopted (or rediscovered) Aristotle's concept of an abstract, not-of-this-universe god, but improved on it. They eliminated the same-stuff-as-us paradox, but unlike Aristotle, the Jew's Yahweh could vanquish enemies, answer their prayers, and be a loving father figure too.

Why is the *Abstract-God* meme so important to the Abrahamic religions? On the surface, it seems like a fairly esoteric topic. The memes we studied earlier had a fairly direct influence on Yahweh's ability to spread and supplant other religion memes. The *Abstract-God* meme is much more subtle: It *supports* the other memes, particularly the *General-Purpose* God meme. It turned Yahweh from a being who was personal and rather human, into something incomprehensible and unknowable. Furthermore, Greek rational philosophy had thrown a spanner in the works by pointing out that God couldn't both create the world *and* be part of it. The *Abstract-God* meme answered these questions by making Yahweh abstract, but with manifestations that were within human comprehension. Yahweh could both create the universe (without being part of it), and participate in the universe.

Although the *Abstract-God* meme was fairly well established before the birth of Jesus, the life and death of Jesus raised this same question all over again, and was a key factor in the first great division of Christianity, called the "Great Schism" or the "East-West Schism" that divided Christians into the Roman and Greek churches. The Roman Emperor Constantine (280-337 AD) is called the first Christian Emperor, although the sincerity of his death-bed acceptance of Christ is questioned by some. During his reign, he ended official persecution of Christians, and declared that all religions were to be tolerated in the Roman Empire. It is likely that his alliance with Christians was political rather than from true faith, but whatever his motives, Christians could, for the first time, worship openly, and could publicly debate the theological details of Christian beliefs.

Most Christians of the third century AD believed that Jesus was divine. But this presented problems, due to the *Abstract God* meme: If Jesus was divine, was he also *human* (same-stuff-as-us), was he *similar nature* to The Father (Yahweh), or was he the *same nature* as The Father? Was Jesus the same as Yahweh, or a separate divine entity? Was he born divine, or promoted to divinity as a sign of Yahweh's favor when he died?

In essence, it reopened the question: Is God a same-stuff-as-us god, or an ethereal god, but this time, the question was for Jesus, not Yahweh.

The debate caused by this seemingly esoteric and unanswerable question was crucial to the Christian community, and caused huge divisions within its ranks. To an outsider, the debate seems impossibly complex, almost absurd, with various sides arguing vigorously about positions that are hard to distinguish from one another. To the Christians, it was at the very heart of their faith.

The Christian Church was by then a powerful force in the empire, and the controversy over the details of Christ's divinity became so heated that Emperor Constantine couldn't ignore it. At first he instructed the church leaders, "... each one of you, showing consideration for the other, listen to the impartial exhortation of your fellow-servant." But the disagreements raged on, and in the year 325 Constantine finally summoned a council of delegates to Nicaea to address the question once and for all. The result was the Nicene Creed, a document that became the foundation of modern Western Christianity, and the Roman Catholic Church in particular. In it, the Council declared that:

> *We believe in one God, the Father Almighty, Maker of all things visible and invisible. And in one Lord Jesus Christ, the Son of God, begotten of the Father [the only-begotten; that is, of the essence of the Father, God of God], Light of Light, very God of very God, begotten, not made, being of one substance with the Father...*

In other words, the "same nature as The Father" faction prevailed. But although the Council of Nicaea issued this creed, the controversy continued. Members of the various factions were sent into exile and then recalled, gained the favor of the emperor and then lost it again.

Five decades later, a second Council at Nicaea was called to once again try to reconcile these questions. The Nicene Creed originally declared that, "We believe in the Holy Spirit, the Lord and Giver of life, who proceeds from the Father..." The Western (Roman) faction inserted the so-called *filioque clause* into the Nicene Creed, changing it to, "... who proceed from the Father *and the Son...*" In other words, Jesus was given equal billing with Yahweh himself, a clear statement of Jesus' divine nature. The Eastern (Greek) Catholic churches disagreed strongly with this view, and 700 years later it became one of the two primary causes of the Great Schism of 1054 AD (the other being Papal authority) that formally divided Catholics into the Greek and Roman Churches.

The *Abstract God* meme was thus transformed down to an earthly level with the life and death of Jesus. It was not an abstract, academic question, but rather was at the very heart of Christianity and the nature of Jesus himself.

The Godly-Origin-of-Morals Meme

Men rarely (if ever) dream up a god superior to themselves.
Most gods have the manners and morals of a spoiled child.
– Robert Heinlein, Time Enough for Love

The greatest tragedy in mankind's entire history may be the
hijacking of morality by religion.
– Arthur C. Clarke

Earlier, we learned about the Amung people of the New Guinean highlands, a people whose beliefs are animistic. The Amung did not have an idea of "gods" that are separate from nature; spirits and nature were one and the same. Their religion wasn't separate from their lives, such as a church that you attend only on Sunday; instead, they were immersed in their religion throughout their lives; their spirits are part of the community rather than separate from it.

Ethics in an animistic society such as the Amung are what you might call *pragmatic*. That is, they develop a code of ethics, but it is not handed down by god. Instead, it develops as a natural part of daily life and a need to maintain order. However, the spirits and natural forces *do* participate in ethics, but as "enforcers" rather than the source of ethics.

Even without a god handing them stone tablets, the Amung have a code of ethics (gathered by Dr. Turinsky Cook through extensive interviews) that is remarkably similar to Western ethics. For example, stealing, lying, adultery, large debts, and sex in sacred places are prohibited, while generosity, gift-giving, sharing, and respect for elders are strongly encouraged. Here is one example of an ethic:

Ethic: *We may not have sexual intercourse with any woman*
we call mother, sister, aunt or with any woman from our
father's moiety.
Sanction: *If a man has committed incest, his gardens will*
not grow and his pigs will die. The same curse will be on
his extended family and lineage. The punishment of incest is
death. His own brothers will kill him to free the family of
the curse. The violators are thrown into the river after
being killed with many arrows. Their blood must not spill
on the land.

Notice that, unlike Christianity, the rewards and punishment are
immediate, not deferred until the afterlife. The villagers are strongly
motivated to carry out the punishment, because if they don't, the
spirits will see to it that *their* gardens don't grow and *their* livestock
dies. But more importantly, there is no mention of ethics *originating*
from the spirits. They're not god-given, but rather are just natural,
pragmatic ethics that the community (including spirits) agree upon.
The Amung make no mention of the origin of their ethics, they
simply learn them as children from the village elders and the story-
tellers.

There is a nearly universal belief held by Christian, Jewish and
Muslim societies around the world: Ethics come from God. It wasn't
always so. Societies like the Amung of New Guinea demonstrate
what appears to be a typical pattern for animistic and pre-monothe-
istic societies – their ethics come from pragmatic rules that the
people develop over time to get along with one another and to
resolve disputes. The *Godly Origin Of Morals* meme states that God
(or the gods) is the only legitimate source of ethics, and the corollary, that humans aren't capable of figuring out what's right and
wrong without help from God.

The *Godly Origin Of Morals* meme appears to have developed
about three to four thousand years ago. Hammurabi (1810 - 1750
BCE) was the sixth king of Babylon, and through expansion via conquests, became the first king of the Babylonian Empire. Hammurabi
believed he was chosen to deliver the gods' laws to humans. Just

before his death, the Babylonian sun god Shamash is said to have handed him a set of 282 laws, which are now known as the Code of Hammurabi. He had these laws inscribed on a huge stone slab, which was very symbolic; Hammurabi was in effect saying, "The laws from the gods can not be changed, even by a king."

Roughly 600 years later, the best known god-given laws, now called the Ten Commandments, were given to Moses by Yahweh (around 1200 BCE). After Moses, both the prophets Jesus and Mohammad extended and created new laws, in both cases said to come directly from Yahweh himself. The life of Jesus was dedicated to teaching ethical lessons to his followers, and many of his sermons are documented in the Christian Bible. The Qur'an contains ethics of Islam, and is said to have been inspired by Yahweh speaking through the Prophet Muhammad over a period of twenty-three years.

Here is an example that illustrates the firm hold the *Godly Origin Of Morals* meme has in the modern Abrahamic religions. Although this is from the Catholic Encyclopedia, it is representative of the views of most Jews, Christians and Muslims.

> *On the other hand, the Church has ever affirmed that [morality and Theism] are essentially connected, and that apart from religion the observance of the moral law is impossible.*
> *– Catholic Encyclopedia (1913)*

In other words, without guidance from Yahweh, there can be no morality.

In addition to the *pragmatic* ethics of early societies, and *god-given* ethics, a third source of ethics arose with the Greeks, that is, Greek Rationalism. The works of Socrates, Plato, Aristotle and the other great Greek philosophers had a profound influence on world history, and were taught in Athens for almost a thousand years, until the Catholic emperor Justinian I closed down all non-Christian schools of philosophy.

The Greek Rationalists deduced that virtue and vice could be defined by a logical chain that began with human happiness, tempered by what today we know as the "Golden Rule." The phrase "everything in moderation" captures it best, but with a critical caveat: Both words, *everything*, and *moderation*, must be adhered to. They defined virtue as the balance between extremes: Bravery was a virtue to be found between rashness and cowardice. Neither the drunk, nor the person who doesn't drink is virtuous, virtue comes from enjoying wine in moderation. Neither the glutton nor the anorexic is virtuous, virtue comes from eating a variety of foods in moderation. The virtuous patriot doesn't defend his country blindly and without question, nor does he run at the first sign of trouble.

Let's return to our brief history of the *Godly Origin of Morals* meme. We've already mentioned the collision of Greek and Jewish cultures during the first millennium BC. This was a critical time for the *Godly Origin of Morals* meme.

The Jews had never encountered this sort of rational thought, but happily for the Jews, the *Anti-Rationalism* meme was also developing, a topic we'll discuss extensively later in the book. The *Anti-Rationalism* meme declares that faith, not logic, is the foundation of true understanding. It gave the Jews a way to reject the Greek Rational arguments about the *Godly Origin of Morals* meme and ignore the logical circularity that the Rationalists discovered. And the rest, as they say, is history: Virtually all Jews, Muslims and Christians today believe that morality can only originate with Yahweh.

The history of Greek Rational philosophy didn't end with the rise of Christianity, although it "hibernated" for a very long time. The *Godly Origin of Morals* meme dominated Western philosophy and religion for almost a thousand years. Greek Rationalism was nearly forgotten, until it finally came out of hibernation during the Renaissance as the Greek writings were rediscovered and reprinted. Rationalism became a real force with the rise of *humanism*, a philosophy based on the ability to determine ethical questions via rational thought and on the human condition. Humanism had a rough time of it at first, being branded "dangerous," but it gained adherents through the nineteenth and twentieth centuries. Today, humanists have several large organizations, web sites, and political groups in America, and are popular enough to regularly draw the wrath of television evangelists and other conservative religious leaders. Humanism has made a revival, and is again a major challenge to the *Godly Origin of Morals* meme.

The Kindness Meme

Cruel men believe in a cruel God and use their belief to excuse their cruelty. Only kindly men believe in a kindly God, and they would be kindly in any case.
– Bertrand Russell (1872-1967)

The earliest versions of gods, being of the same-stuff-as-us variety, also have many human flaws, including the all-too-human emotions of vengeance, anger, and meanness. This makes for great stories and myths, and it isn't much of a problem in polytheistic religions where various gods fill different roles. There's no damage to the theology if the god of war is mean, the god of wine is a drunken partier, or the goddess of love is capricious, promiscuous and fickle.

But as the *All-Purpose* God and *Monotheism* memes started to take hold, these characteristics became a problem. If you only have one god, to whom you look for all of your spiritual needs, you'd like to know that this god will look on you with kindness, a sort of father figure who has your best interests at heart. Consider Zeus: he killed Salmoneus just for impersonating him, he turned Pandareus to stone for stealing, he turned Chelone to a tortoise when she wouldn't attend a wedding, and turned King Haemus and Queen Rhodope into mountains for their vanity. Zeus had a pretty bad temper.

Yahweh was even worse. Dawkins puts it succinctly:

"The God of the Old Testament is arguably the most unpleasant character in all fiction: jealous and proud of it; a petty, unjust, unforgiving control-freak; a vindictive, bloodthirsty ethnic cleanser; a misogynistic, homophobic, racist, infanticidal, genocidal, filicidal, pestilential, megalomaniacal, sadomasochistic, capriciously malevolent bully."

And it's no joke – any scholar of the Old Testament can almost immediately recognize exactly which chapter and verse Dawkins is talking about. Jealous? See the First Commandment. Bloodthirsty? Read Deuteronomy, Exodus and a dozen other books. Genocide? Filicide? Pestilence? It's all there, in black and white.

As Armstrong writes:

"This is a brutal, partial and murderous god ... he is passionately partisan, has little compassion for anyone but his own favorites and is simply a tribal deity. If Yahweh had remained such a savage god, the sooner he vanished, the better..."

But Yahweh didn't remain the mean bully of the Old Testament. Armstrong goes on to say:

"... Yahweh did not remain the cruel and violent god of the Exodus ... the Israelites would transform him beyond recognition into a symbol of transcendence and compassion."

This is the essence of the *Kindness* meme: The Yahweh worshipped by Jews, Muslims and Christians around the world today is kind, fair, compassionate and loving. Yahweh is the father we all wished we'd had, one who would keep us in line, give out fair punishment when we're bad, protect us from danger, and above all, love us unconditionally.

This was another critical mutation to the Yahweh memeplex, one that provided important synergy with some of the other memes we've studied. It was not a problem if the Roman Zeus, the Hawai'ian Pele, and the Israelite's old Yahweh, had bad tempers, because their worshippers had other gods to turn to for their emotional needs. The Old Testament's Yahweh Sabaoth, the God of Armies, was *supposed* to be mean. But by the time of Jesus, Yahweh had turned into the abstract, all-purpose god-of-everything, and it just wouldn't do for him to be the jealous, hotheaded god of Abraham's time.

Like the *Abstract God* meme, the *Kindness* meme supports the first three of our memes that transformed Yahweh from a tribal god to the god-of-everything. As the one-and-only god, Yahweh has to be someone you can love and respect, not a god who was no better than an undisciplined, bad-tempered child.

The Asexual Meme

Of the delights of this world, man cares most for sexual intercourse, yet he has left it out of his heaven.
– Mark Twain (1835-1910)

The *Asexual meme* is closely related to the *Kindness* meme we just studied. Early gods, being same-stuff-as-humans, tend to be sexual, capricious, and amoral or immoral. We can look at just about any old religion to see this: Zeus had a pederastic relationship with the young god Ganymede; Zeus also took the form of a swan and raped Leda, the Queen of Sparta, who bore Helen of Troy. In Egyptian mythology, the god Atern masturbated to produce the twins Shu and Tefnut, and the lovers Nut (goddess of the sky) and her brother Geb (god of the earth) were said to be in a constant state of incestual lovemaking. Even Yahweh, the Israelites' god, was believed by many to have a wife – some Israelites thought the Queen of Heaven (Isis/Ishtar), goddess of love, was the wife of Yahweh.

While sex is not amoral or immoral *per se*, the sexuality of gods is usually associated with other flaws, such as rape, jealousy, incest, pedophilia, and all the other human transgressions that go with sexuality. This became a problem as Yahweh evolved, particularly in light of the *Godly Origin of Morals* meme. If Yahweh was handing down the Ten Commandments to Moses, he had to be above reproach himself.

The *Asexuality* meme is actually somewhat of a corollary to the *Abstract God* meme, in that it's natural when a same-stuff-as-us god morphs into a more abstract and less human god, that god would naturally lose other human traits such as sexuality. Even so, it is a separate and important concept, that Yahweh lost his sexuality over the millennia, and we need to understand it as a meme in its own right.

In a later chapter, we'll also see how the *Asexuality* meme is critically important to some Christians, such as the conservative American churches, who have a view that sex is inherently sinful. For these Christians, their theology is completely incompatible with a sexual Yahweh.

By becoming asexual, Yahweh gained the "moral high ground" in that, unlike Zeus and his ilk, Yahweh could never commit any sexual sins. Thus, the *Asexuality* meme supports the *Godly Origin of Morals* meme, because a god who hands us our morals must himself be above reproach.

The Synergy of the Eight Memes

Only strength can cooperate. Weakness can only beg.
– Dwight D. Eisenhower

We've seen eight trends in religion memes. Let us quickly review them, and examine how these eight trends, or "lines of meme mutations," are synergistic.

- Specialist god to general-purpose god
- Polytheism to monotheism
- Tolerance of other gods to intolerance
- Local gods to global gods
- Physical ("same stuff as us") to abstract
- Pragmatic/natural ethics to god-given rules
- Unlikable to kind
- Sexual to asexual

If we "go back in time" in our minds four thousand years, before most of the meme mutations in the list above had begun, the importance of these eight memes becomes clear. Take any one of the gods of Abraham's time: Isis, Yahweh (Abraham's El, not the modern God Almighty), Baal, Asherah, or Anat, and ask yourself: Could this god have become as popular and widely worshipped as the God Almighty that the Christians, Muslims and Jews worship today?

The answer should be an emphatic, *No!* Those old gods simply didn't have what it took to achieve "stardom," to take on the whole world. There were too many of them, each one served only a few of our needs, they were tied to particular regions, they not only tolerated each other but were not even jealous of each other, some (such as Yahweh himself) were petulant, unlikable bullies, they were immoral or amoral, and they offered little or no ethical guidance. On top of all that, they were susceptible to challenges from rational thinkers such as Plato.

Each one of the eight trends above, by itself, was important. But like evolution in the world of plants and animals, it takes more than one thing to make a species dominant. Mutations, whether of memes or of genes, are synergistic and build on one another. The large human brain, for example, is important, but by itself, a big brain wouldn't have resulted in human domination of Earth. However, when a large brain is combined with bipedal locomotion, opposable thumbs, language, omnivorism, and various other traits, the combination results in humans dominating the Earth.

Similarly, each of the trends in the religion memes, and in the Yahweh meme in particular, is important, but it is the synergy that results from all eight trends that ultimately made Yahweh the one god of the Western world, the one we call God.

Interlude: The Big V

The turtle lives 'twixt plated decks
Which practically conceal its sex.
I think it clever of the turtle
In such a fix to be so fertile.
– Ogden Nash

Engineers, especially software engineers, have a reputation for being geeks. Nerds. A bit clueless about women and socializing. Frustratingly even-tempered, not showing a lot of emotion even when life throws them some curve balls. Newfound love or a relationship on the rocks, our team winning the World Series or losing it, a big bonus at work or a layoff ... these things all send their more artistic / emotive friends to the heights of happiness or the pits of despair, while the engineer just keeps sailing along on an even keel.

In college, one of my engineering professors told us of a faculty meeting where an English professor accused him of being a "linear thinker." We all sat there waiting for the punch line, until he explained to us that the English professor considered this an insult. Now THAT was funny – that straight, logical path to an optimal solution was an insult! Then someone asked, "Does the English professor advocate circular logic?" Which brought on more laughter. We were geeks one and all.

I'm happy to report that this *Engineers-Are-Geeks* meme, is ... true. Plain and simple, it's the reality. I've worked with a LOT of engineers – mechanical, electrical, chemical, civil, and software engineers – and I'll state without hesitation that engineers are pretty geeky. No, they didn't all have plastic pocket protectors, and they didn't all wear button-down collars. Some of them were excellent musicians, expert jugglers, great racing sailors, or fanatical motorcycle riders. But they all shared that core element of "linear thinking" that works so well in engineering, and (unfortunately for their less geeky friends and loved ones) they carry this mindset over into their personal lives.

Which is why, in the Spring of 1982, I was caught completely off guard, blindsided by a deep and unexpected, and completely irrational, emotional experience. My life, which had always sailed on its even keel, was hit an emotional storm so powerful it was knocked sideways, its gunwales awash. The cause of this hurricane of emotions was a tiny bundle containing a mere seven pounds of baby. My attraction to this bundle was fierce and primitive, way down deep inside me, of an intensity I'd never experienced before. Sure, I'd felt love, lust, disappointment, happiness and anger before. But nothing like this primordial, naked pull of nature, telling me, "THAT'S YOUR CHILD." The bond was immediate. I knew, right then and there, that I'd willingly stand in harms way, or even give my life, to protect my baby. I had never, ever, felt anything even remotely as intense and primitive as I felt in those minutes.

I'd always thought this sort of bonding experience was for mothers, not fathers, and my linear way of thinking made me completely unprepared for this wonderful, instinctive and utterly non-linear emotional experience. I was more prepared when my second and third children were born, but still felt that wonderful love that only a child can inspire.

Eighteen years later, I faced another primitive emotional storm. During those eighteen years, my three wonderful kids grew into young adults, my career and hobbies expanded, and I was beginning to look forward to the days when my child-rearing duties were complete. I only had to deliberate briefly before I concluded that I didn't need any more children in my life, which meant it was time for me to visit the urologist for the Big V – that is, to get a vasectomy.

Once again, I was unexpectedly overwhelmed by non-linear, irrational thinking. What should have been a completely logical course of action, to end my fertility, proved to be remarkably difficult in practice. Sure, I knew all the funny jokes comparing sterilization to castration, and these didn't bother me; my intellectual, rational side was still intact enough to know that my manliness wasn't threatened.

It was deeper than that. The idea that I shouldn't have more children was easy to accept, but the I idea that I *couldn't* have more children, ever ... I just didn't want to do that. My rational side knew that I'd never father another child. My primitive side didn't want to give up. Somewhere, deep inside me, there was still that most basic instinct telling me, "Reproduce!" My intellectual brain was exceptionally good at converting this primitive voice into convincing excuses. "Maybe," it whispered to me, "your whole family will be killed in a car wreck, and you'll need to start again!" Or, "I hear there are lots of side effects to the operation! You could get cysts, and groin pain!" Or, "It's the woman who gets pregnant, let her take care of it!"

My primitive primate brain isn't very smart, and I hate it when it wins arguments. So, I finally told it to shut up, went to the urologist, and got it over with. But it wasn't easy.

3. Evolution and Memes

When Does Information Become a Meme?

Thus, from the war of nature, from famine and death, the most exalted object which we are capable of conceiving, namely, the production of the higher animals, directly follows.
– Charles Darwin (1809-1882)

Up to this point, we have had just a very brief introduction to memes and memetics, with a few examples to illustrate the basics and get the idea across. We then jumped straight into our analysis of religion's history up to the time of Jesus. Before we continue with our history and analysis, we need to take a more detailed look at memetics, really study it, to learn in some detail how the principles of evolution apply to culture and ideas. What is it that makes memes so much like genes, and to what extent do they differ? Is memetics really a deep insight into cultural evolution, or are the parallels between genes and memes just an amusing coincidence?

In the introductory chapters, we learned how cultural information, called memes, seems to be very analogous to genetic information. By "stepping back" from Darwin's principles and looking at genes as information rather than as DNA, we learned how Darwin's principles, under the right circumstances, can apply to other types of information besides genetic information – in particular, to memes.

The term "under the right circumstances" is the key: What are those circumstances? Information comes in a huge variety of forms and content, everything from terabytes of astronomical data streaming from a radiotelescope, to beautiful songs, to the 5,000 year old cuneiform clay tablets of Sumeria. Most information is *not* memetic, that is, it does not replicate itself, nor is it shaped by evolutionary forces. But some information does. We need to identify the conditions required for cultural evolution to do its work, for a piece of information to become a meme.

Reproduction

I have sinned against you, and I beg your forgiveness.
-- Jimmy Swaggert, Christian Television Evangelist, to his
wife, after being photographed taking a prostitute to a Loui-
siana motel.

To survive, evolve, and compete, every living thing from the smallest retrovirus to the monstrous Blue Whale, the largest animal ever to live on the Earth (and still around today), must reproduce.

In April of 1991, Mr. and Mrs. Smith (not their real names), the young parents of a beautiful daughter, found themselves sitting across the table from investigators in the United States Attorney's office, embarrassed at answering questions about something they thought was completely private. The Smiths had gone to see Dr. Jacobson, an infertility doctor, because they weren't able to conceive a child on their own, and had finally opted for artificial insemination by an anonymous sperm donor. The federal investigators were very polite, and apologized for causing the Smiths embarrassment. But they wanted to know if the Smiths could please answer a few questions about Dr. Jacobson's infertility program. Why had the Smiths sought out Dr. Jacobsen? What had he told them about his infertility program? Had they become pregnant from Dr. Jacobsen's treatment?

Although it took a while, due to privacy and ethics concerns, the truth was finally revealed to the Smiths, and to dozens of other patients. Dr. Cecil B. Jacobson had apparently decided that the eight children he'd fathered with his wife weren't enough. Instead of using sperm from anonymous donors, matched to the Mr. Smith's physical characteristics, Dr. Jacobson had used his own sperm to impregnate Mrs. Smith and the other patients who came to him for infertility treatment. In some cases where the husband was able to use his own sperm for *in vitro* fertilization, Dr. Jacobson had simply discarded the husband's sperm, substituting his own.

Many of Dr. Jacobson's patients who were contacted by the U.S. Attorney's office were reluctant to have their children's DNA tested, so the final count is uncertain, but it's likely that Dr. Jacobson had fathered, via his fraudulent artificial inseminations, sixty to eighty children. Dr. Jacobson was ultimately convicted of fraud and perjury, and for causing his patients "extreme psychological injury." He was sentenced to five years in prison, three years of probation, and fined $117,000.

All men have a strong desire for sex, which (before the advent of birth control) would often result in the impregnation of their sex partner. All human traits vary, including our desire to reproduce. Dr. Jacobson simply took this drive to the extreme, using technology to father many dozens of children.

Even in more normal cases, the birth of a child is almost always the cause for congratulations to the father, even though his role in the process is quite enjoyable, particularly compared to the woman's job. We are genetically programmed to appreciate and be proud of our children. We have a very strong drive to reproduce.

The most fundamental requirement for an evolutionary process is that the information being reproduced (whether a meme, a virus, or an elephant) must carry within it the motivation or mechanism that triggers its own reproduction. This is deceptively simple on the surface: Living things reproduce, and memes reproduce. But the mechanisms are amazingly varied. In the case of viruses and bacteria, the mechanisms are purely biochemical: At some point, certain carefully timed biochemical reactions are triggered, which starts the process of replication (viruses) or splitting (bacteria). On the other end of the scale, humans, elephants and whales have a much more intricate set of genes that code for their reproductive organs, and other genes that control the behavioral patterns of sexual attraction and mating. But whether it's a simple biochemical sequence for a virus, or a complex twenty-year process for a human that starts with courtship and marriage and ends when the offspring are themselves sexually mature, the common feature, from the smallest living thing to the largest, is that the reproductive act is *controlled by the genes.* That is, the information (genome) that is being reproduced contains the instructions for its own reproduction.

In the case of memes, the "motivation" for reproduction is equally varied. We call a friend to warn of a police radar trap in our neighborhood out of altruism or the hope for a reciprocal warning in the future. We pass on a good joke so that our friends and family will enjoy our company and continue to invite us to parties. We tell our children stories of our own youthful mistakes in the hope that they won't repeat them. We indoctrinate our children with our religion, because we believe the benefits of the correct beliefs are magnificent and the penalties for the wrong beliefs are horrifying.

These motivations are all quite different, but like biological life, they all share a common theme: The *meme itself* causes you to want to repeat it, to teach it to someone else. Just like a genome, the meme contains the information that causes its own reproduction. That's what makes it a meme, and not just data.

Survival of the Fittest

> *A scientific man ought to have no wishes, no affections, a mere heart of stone.*
> – Charles Darwin (1809-1882)

James William Tutt, an English entomologist, wrote a really boring book called *Natural History of the British Lepidoptera* (1890-1911). Well, maybe other entomologists find it fascinating, but I fell asleep after a few pages. Ordinarily, a book like Tutt's would be read by a few and then forgotten on some dusty shelf in the university library's attic. But buried among a thousand other dry facts, Tutt reported one of the first, and still one of the best, examples of "survival of the fittest" in action.

In pre-industrial England, the peppered moths (*Biston betularia*) were almost all light colored – about ninety-eight percent were white with dark "pepper" specks, and two percent were dark with light specks, and by good luck (and hard work) this statistic had been carefully documented by scientists. The light-colored moths blended exceptionally well with the lichen-covered trees on which they landed, making them hard for birds to spot.

The industrial revolution in England brought textiles, transportation, food production, manufactured goods – just about every aspect of life was changed. But it had a price: Between 1800 and 1900, the energy used by England increased tenfold, and this energy came almost entirely from burning coal, vast quantities of it. The resulting sooty pollution killed the lichens and blackened the trees on which the peppered moths like to land. The light-colored moths who landed on these soot-covered trees were easy for birds to spot, and the dark moths were well hidden. The result? In just forty-seven years, the dark-colored moth population grew from from two percent to ninety-eight percent, a complete reversal of the percentages.

J.W. Tutt's discovery and explanation was a dramatic and simple example of "survival of the fittest" in action, one that has become a textbook case, studied by virtually all students of evolution. It shows, literally in "black and white," just how powerful the filtering process of natural selection can be.

"Survival of the Fittest" is the best-known part of Darwin's principles, and has become somewhat of a popular shorthand for Darwin's entire thesis. The cheetah who runs faster catches more food and raises more fast baby cheetahs. The frog whose tongue is longer and stickier catches more flies, and has more baby frogs with longer, stickier tongues. The smallpox virus that does *not* kill you quickly will have more opportunities to infect other people, so it spreads faster. These are the "fittest," the ones that go on to reproduce and create the most copies of their genes.

But here's the problem: Both "survival" and "fittest" are misleading terms!

The word "fittest" conjures up ideas of wholesomeness, athletic prowess, morality and other human values. Nothing could be further from the truth: Evolution doesn't care about human concepts like "right" and "wrong" or "good" and "bad." It's unfortunate that the word "fittest," which brings so many human moral and ethical connotations, is a keyword of Evolution Science. It's not "fitness" that matters, it's "reproduction." To put this in human terms, Mormons and Catholics are more "fit" than atheists and others, because they typically have more children.

The word "survival" is misleading, too. The male black widow spider knows this all too well: The female bites his head off during mating, and consumes his body afterwards. Survival isn't the relevant term – reproduction is all that matters. The male black widow spider reproduces very effectively, in spite of not surviving at all. It's his DNA that survives.

We could try to coin a more descriptive term, perhaps something like "the correlation between specific genetic characteristics and reproductive success." This doesn't offer any moral or ethical judgement on whether a trait is wise or foolish, moral or immoral, ethical or unethical, good or bad. But, such a phrase will never stick – it's boring and hard to decipher. By contrast, "survival of the fittest" is a very successful phrase, because of the very thing that makes it inaccurate. The phrase has drama ("survival") and it has a sort of good-versus-evil feel ("fittest"). Humans love a good story, and this simple phrase is evocative. As a meme, "survival of the fittest" is much more fit for survival than other phrases that might not have so many moral/ethical connotations! It's a perfect illustration of a core theme in this book, that the entities that reproduce more (whether they are jokes, malaria, or elephants) are the ones that become the most common, irrespective of anything else.

What do the following have in common?

There are alligators living in the New York sewers, and they got there because people bought cute baby alligators, but flushed them down the toilet when they grew too large.

Einstein's Theory of Relativity says you can't go faster than the speed of light.

"Knock knock." "Who's there?" ...

God gave Moses ten commandments, chiseled into two stone tablets.

Princess Diana was assassinated by the British Royal family because she was about to marry a non-Christian foreigner.

There is an inexpensive tablet that can be added to water that makes it as powerful as gasoline, but the oil companies have suppressed this knowledge because it would put them out of business.

Cool stuff, right? But are they true? More importantly, *does it matter if these ideas are true?* No! Some are true, some are false, and some are outrageous lies. Each of these ideas originated in the mind of (at least) one person, was told, and retold, and possibly changed along the way, and *survived*. It doesn't matter *why* it survived and was retold, only that it did.

This is survival of the fittest in the classic sense. Each of these memes, for unique reasons, was an idea that most people found *more interesting* or *funnier,* than the other competing urban myths and jokes. Each of these memes is a *survivor*. For each one of these, there were millions, perhaps billions of ideas that popped into some-one's head, but never got further than that. You have an idea: "I think I'll go to the store." You may or may not mention it to anyone else, but even if you do, it's just not interesting enough. It just dies there, and never spreads to the next person. By contrast, when someone tells you "I heard that Princess Diana was killed because...," you think "Wow! That's fascinating!" And because it's a morbidly fascinating meme, one that suggests the high-and-mighty are no better than common criminals (never mind that it's a cruel lie), you pass it on.

Mutation

Consistency requires you to be as ignorant today as you were a year ago.
– Bernard Berenson (1865-1959)

A couple with whom I am very close, call them Peter and Lacy (not their real names), had the good fortune to find themselves pregnant and were ecstatic about it. But, like many pregnancies, theirs ended early when the Lacy felt ill, experienced severe cramps, and had a miscarriage. Although they were saddened by this all-too-common tragedy, they were determined to let Lacy rest, recover, and try again.

This would have been the end to a sad but otherwise common story, but for one thing. About six weeks later, Lacy went to her gynecologist for what was supposed to be her "all clear" visit, so that Peter and Lacy could try again for another pregnancy. Before the doctor began the examination, he asked Lacy, "How are you feeling? Have you recovered emotionally from your difficult miscarriage?" Lacy got a perplexed look on her face. "Doctor, I know this sounds crazy ... I know for certain I had a miscarriage ... but ... well, I think I'm still pregnant!" And indeed she was. Lacy had been carrying twins, and only one of the two miscarried; instead of getting green light for more fun in the marital bed, Peter and Lacy got the wonderful news that Lacy was three months pregnant.

Six months later, they had a beautiful, healthy boy. Today as I write these words, their son is quite a handsome young man, just about to graduate from high school. His biggest problem is trying to decide which of the top universities he wants to attend, since several have offered him entrance.

Doctors have always known that ten to twenty percent of women who learn they are pregnant have a miscarriage, so it's not surprising that occasionally, one of a pair of twins will miscarry and the other remain healthy.

When high-resolution ultrasound and modern pregnancy tests came on the scene, it was possible to detect pregnancy much earlier and with high accuracy, and doctors found that the real rate of miscarriage is probably around 30% or more of all pregnancies. Many women have a miscarriage without even knowing they are pregnant. Geneticists were able to detect that at least forty percent of miscarriages were caused by readily identifiable chromosomal abnormalities. In all likelihood, a large fraction of the remaining sixty percent are also caused by more subtle genetic problems.

We tend to think that our genetic material is pretty rugged, that we manage to pass it on our genes to our children reliably. After all, our kids look like us, right? But as illustrated by the story of Peter and Lacy's miscarriage, the facts are otherwise: Reproduction is a tricky business, with a high rate of errors. In fact, studies of the human genome suggest that we each carry something like one hundred mutations on our genome! (This is a very rough number and still being researched, but the point is: It's a lot of mutations.) Most of these are harmless or only slightly detrimental, as otherwise the human race would have died out long ago.

Mutations of the genome have a conflicting dual role in evolution: They're both good and bad. On the one hand, they're almost never beneficial, so over a short period of time, it's far better for a species to have a highly stable (non mutating) genome. On the other hand, mutation creates variability, and variations enable a species to adapt to changes in the environment, new predators, diseases, and a host of other threats that could wipe it out. So, while mutations are "bad" for the individual, they are necessary for the long-term survival of a species.

Mutation is perhaps the most misunderstood aspect of Darwin's Evolution Science, and is the target of most attacks on evolution by those who claim Darwin was wrong. And with good reason: Until recently, the biochemistry, physics, and statistical mechanisms of mutation were not well understood. It was a huge weakness in Evolution Science. Scientists waved their hands and claimed, "Over billions of years, there have been enough 'good' mutations to cause the primordial soup to evolve into humans. And the proof is that we exist, so it must be true!" It was a circular argument.

But happily, science doesn't sit still. Mutation can be observed by scientists, and the hand-waving has been replaced by a solid body of science proving that the hypothesized mutations really do occur, and they really do drive evolution. Evolution Science's weak point has been dramatically strengthened as scientists learned the complex biochemistry of DNA and reproduction. We now understand how DNA works, how it copies itself, what can go wrong in the process, and especially, how DNA protects itself via repair systems, redundancy, and with immune systems that recognize and destroy damaged cells.

(I must warn readers that I'm playing fast and loose with terms like "DNA", "genes," "genome" and "mutation" and many other scientific terms. There are very important distinctions between genes, a genome, and DNA. A true understanding of how evolution works requires a much deeper treatment than I have room for here.)

Memes, like genes, are subject to mutation. They can survive an amazing variety of retellings and still retain their central concept, their meme-ness. Consider...

Version 1:

> In Heaven, Saint Peter is giving a guided tour to a group of new arrivals. "You're going to like it here," he says, "we have a place just for you." He takes them down a hall and opens the first door. Inside, there's a big party, with everyone drinking wine and dancing. "These are the Catholics. Boy do they know how to party!" he says. Moving to the next door, he opens it, revealing a more serious group, with everyone arguing and gesturing. "And here are the Jews, they like to talk." Walking further, they reach the next door, which St. Peter opens to reveal a room full of card tables, with various games of bingo and cards in progress. "The Lutherans!" says St. Peter. But at the next door, St. Peter stops them and says, "Ok, now you must be very quiet." He opens the door just a crack, and whispers, "These are the Baptists. They think they're the only ones here."

Version 2:

> A man arrives at the gates of heaven. St. Peter asks, "Religion?" The man says, "Methodist." St. Peter looks down his list, and says, "Go to room 24, but be very quiet as you pass room 8."
>
> Another man arrives at the gates of heaven. "Religion?" "Baptist." "Go to room 18, but be very quiet as you pass room 8."

A third man arrives at the gates. "Religion?" "Jewish." "Go to room 11, but be very quiet as you pass room 8." The man says, "I can understand there being different rooms for different religions, but why must I be quiet when I pass room 8?" St. Peter tells him, "Well the Catholics are in room 8, and they think they're the only ones here."

What is the meme here? The specific telling of the joke varies widely, but the punch line is always the same: Some particular church thinks they have the exclusive key to heaven, and St. Peter is humoring them. The meme is the *concept*, not the specific words used to convey the concept. A particular meme can be expressed in many, many ways and still retain its identity.

This brings us to an important difference between genes and memes: A concept, the core idea that is being conveyed via the meme, can be expressed in a variety of different ways. For example, a Catholic priest could teach the catechism in Italian, English, German, Japanese, Hawaiian, or any one of hundreds of other languages, and the core concepts of the catechism memes would be nearly identical. In other words, we must be careful to distinguish between *changes in the message* (the concept), and *changes in the medium* (the particular words used to convey the concept).

This is actually true of genes, too. In most cases the medium (the DNA sequence) and the message (the protein it encodes) are tightly coupled, but there are examples of different DNA sequences that code for the same protein. However, this doesn't alter the main point here: The medium (words) and message (concept) are much more distinct for a meme than for a gene.

Both the medium and the message can affect the survival of the meme. The concept itself can be so appealing that it can be expressed in many ways and still spread; the message (the specific words) may not be important. We see that in the previous joke about Saint Peter – the particular retelling wasn't as important as the central concept.

On the other hand, a well-crafted medium can make an otherwise uninteresting meme become widespread. Advertising firms know this all too well: They purposely wrap uninteresting memes ("buy our product!") inside of an interesting message, such as a nice song, a humorous advertisement, or a sexually provocative image.

This leads us to the other key difference between memes and genes. Until very recently, genes only changed by random mutation; beneficial mutations were rare, and evolution was a glacially slow process. By contrast, memes sometimes mutate randomly (poor memory in the teller, or a misunderstanding of the concept), but they are often altered deliberately, by someone with a specific goal. Because of this, meme evolution is orders of magnitude faster than genetic evolution.

Note that I said "until very recently" when asserting that genes only mutate by random processes. One of the most interesting developments in the history of life on Earth is that scientist are now able to *deliberately* modify genes, and to do so with precision. An early example was when scientists learned to transfer the genes for the luciferase enzyme responsible for the firefly's glow into other creatures such as mice, causing parts of the mice to glow faintly when certain genes are activated.

And one of the most ironic twists of all was the development of the first transgenic plant. Scientist had assured the public that transgenic experiments could help feed humankind by making crops more productive and nutritious, or grow in harsher climates, or be more pest resistant so that farmers could use organic techniques. But when the first transgenic plant was announced, environmentalists were horrified: The plant was altered so that it could withstand *more* herbicides. Glycophosphate, a potent herbicide, was being used for weed control in farming, but it has the not-surprising tendency to destroy crops too. So the scientists grafted genes from a petunia, which is resistant to glycophosphate, into other crops, which made it possible for the farmers to *increase* the use of glycophosphate on their crops.

This illustrates how genes have become more like memes, subject to deliberate change by design. Beneficial traits can be added, and detrimental genes can be removed. The pace of evolution, which for 3.5 billion years has followed a slow, predictable pattern, has been freed from its constraints in a single generation. It is this author's opinion that this will be one of the most significant event in the history of life on Earth. Only time will tell.

Wrestling with God

Kill one man and you are a murderer. Kill millions and you are a conqueror. Kill all and you are a God.
– Jean Rostand

An excellent example of meme mutation is the revision of Yahweh's visit to Abraham. In Abraham's time, those who worshipped Yahweh believed he was a "same stuff as humans" sort of god, made of flesh and blood, but with god-like powers. It was perfectly reasonable to think such a god could sit down with Abraham, and it wasn't surprising that Abraham took a while to figure out that his guest was Yahweh. But a few thousand years later, the Yahweh meme had evolved – now Yahweh was such a mighty god that his presence would be unbearable to a mere human. So how can we explain Abraham's visitor? By mutations of the memes that explain Yahweh's presence at Abraham's table.

At any particular moment in history, different explanations of Abraham's visitor would be put forth. Some variations of the Abraham story were undoubtedly better, that is, more consistent with the more exalted Yahweh, and thus were more likely to be retold. Others were inconsistent and led to "mental tension" in people who wanted to believe the stories in the Bible. Naturally, the more appealing memes were the ones that reconciled this problem.

This is classical "survival of the fittest" or "natural selection." In the end, the new interpretation is that Yahweh didn't appear in person to Abraham, but instead sent a manifestation of himself, something that was tolerable to Abraham's earthly flesh. The mutation and filtering process did its work, allowing Yahweh to become almighty without discarding the story of Abraham's visitor.

Overpopulation

> *The most dreadful thing of all is that many millions of people in the poor countries are going to starve to death before our eyes. We shall see them doing so upon our television sets.*
> *– Charles Percy Snow (1905-1980)*

One of the surprising facts about evolution is that *overpopulation is an integral part of the process.* Without overpopulation, natural selection (survival of the fittest) would be irrelevant.

Let's say, for illustration, that a bunch of rabbits live in a particular region, and half of those rabbits, by chance, have slightly longer fur. By bad luck, a climate change comes along, bringing many decades of colder weather. Now suppose that the short-haired rabbits are just one percent more likely to die in the cold than the longer-haired rabbits, and because of this, for every hundred long-haired rabbits that survive, only ninety-nine short-hair rabbits survive. That hardly seems important, does it? Even after ten generations, there is only a drop of ten percent in the short-haired rabbit population. But that one percent keeps doing its work, generation after generation. By the fiftieth generation (which can be well under fifty years), the short-haired rabbits' population is down by forty percent, and at one hundred generations, only a third of the short-haired rabbits remain. In a thousand generations, a mere blink of the eye on the geological timescale, the short-haired rabbits are practically extinct.

Now imagine we could go back, and conduct this same experiment but in a place where there are no limits, a magical rabbit *Shangri La* where there is plenty to eat, no predators, and room for the rabbit population to grow and grow. The "better" rabbits would breed slightly faster, but the "lesser" rabbits would still survive. There would be no filtering, no selection; all varieties of the rabbits would thrive. With enough food, and enough space, even some very "unfit" rabbits, perhaps with birth defects or other weaknesses, could easily reproduce; their genes would not become extinct.

In this rabbit's Shangri La, even a cold century wouldn't necessarily make the short-haired rabbits extinct. Their numbers would grow more slowly than the long-haired rabbits, *but it wouldn't matter* – the short-haired rabbits' genes would keep on reproducing, making more copies of itself. "Survival of the Fittest" only matters when some individuals don't survive.

A corollary to this is that *all* species on Earth tend to overpopulate. The above-mentioned rabbits can, under the right conditions, have as many as five litters each year; a single mother can have thirty-five offspring in a single year. Spiders lay a sac of eggs that can hatch thousands of baby spiders. The salmon swims upstream and lays several *thousand* eggs. Since all species on Earth have fairly static populations over a long period of time, it is clear that most of these offspring don't live to maturity; on average, of the thousands of baby spiders that hatch, or the thousands of salmon hatchlings, only one will reach maturity and have offspring of its own.

This overpopulation is required for evolution to do its work. In each generation, far more babies are born than can survive, and they're not all identical. This is the raw material that feeds the relentless filter of natural selection.

As you might by now expect, this same principle applies to memes: Overpopulation is the key to evolution. Let us return to our favorite, the lowly joke, to illustrate. I have no idea how many jokes are running around the United States right now, but I would be surprised if it is more than 100,000 at any one time, in fact, I'd be surprised if there are more than 10,000 "active" jokes at any given time.

There are two primary limitations on a joke's ability to reproduce. First, there are only a few billion people in the world; once these brains are all "full" of jokes, there isn't room for more. Some jokes will be forgotten as new ones are told.

Second, unless you are a professional comedian, you probably only spend a small fraction of your life telling jokes. I'd be surprised if each of you readers has told more than two jokes today, and most of you haven't told any jokes today. So jokes not only compete for "room" in your brain, they also compete for very limited "reproduction time." Overpopulation has the exact same role in the Darwinistic analysis of jokes (and all memes) as it does in biological evolution.

There are far more ideas generated each day, and variations on existing ideas, than can possibly survive in the long run. The relentless filtering of natural selection works on memes, just as it works on genes, by filtering out the less fit memes, and passing on the more fit memes as they are retold and "grow" in a new mind.

The Ideosphere and Niches

Forgive, O Lord, my little jokes on Thee, and
I'll forgive Thy great big joke on me.
– Robert Frost (1874-1963)

How about this joke:

I got my mother a book about atheism for Christmas.

I like this joke, but you may not – perhaps you're not a fan of irony, or perhaps you don't like to make fun of Christmas. Either way, this joke has a limited audience compared to many.

In the biological world, each species has a *niche*, a place in the ecological system where it can survive. Giant redwood trees get almost half their water from fog, so they thrive in the foggy Pacific Northwest, but can't survive in the heat of Southern California where the palm trees grow. Trout live in fresh water, and are poisoned by salt water. Penguins thrive in the cold, and die of overheating in even a moderate climate. Some very slow-growing bacteria even live deep inside of rocks, thousands of feet below ground.

A species' niche is the specific range of conditions under which it can live. It includes the basic environment (water, land, air, inside rocks), temperature, food sources, salinity, acidity, water supply and any other environmental factor that affects the species' ability to survive and reproduce.

Every species' niche has limits. It may be the entire Pacific Ocean for a whale, or a tiny pond for a fresh-water guppie. Whichever it is, the environment limits the number of individuals that can survive. The ocean fills up with whales, the pond with guppies, at which point not all of the babies born will survive to adulthood.

What about memes? Consider and contrast these two jokes:

A rope gets drunk and disheveled and all tangled up, and walks into a bar. The bartender takes one look at the rope and says, "Hey! We don't serve ropes here. Are you a rope?" The rope replies, "No, I'm a frayed knot!"

René Descartes walks into a bar. The bartender asks, "Will you have a drink?" Descartes replies, "I don't think..." and *poof* disappears.

The first one has wide appeal; in fact, I suspect many of my readers have heard it already (or a variant). But don't be surprised if you've never heard the second one, or if you don't get it. It's a philosopher's joke. Descartes was the great philosopher and mathematician whose most-quoted line is, "I think, therefore I am," which he asserted proved his own existence.

Jokes and other memes live in your brain, just as a fish lives in water. The "world" for memes consists of the collective set of all brains in the world. Douglas Hofstadter coined the term *ideosphere* for this. The ideosphere is the collective intelligence of all humans, and is the environment in which memes live, reproduce, compete, and mutate.

Within the ideosphere, there are niches, just like the niches of the biological world. The first joke above ("frayed knot"), has a large audience: All English-speaking people. But notice that, because it's a play on words, specifically on the fact that "afraid not" and "a frayed knot" sound alike, it can't be translated to other languages so it can't live in the Russian-speaking section of the ideosphere.

The second joke (Descartes) has a much smaller niche: Philosophers, mathematicians, and a few other individuals who know who Descartes was, and exactly what he meant when he said, "I think, therefore I am."

Memeplexes

Truth, in the matters of religion, is simply the opinion that has survived.
– Oscar Wilde (1854-1900)

Imagine I said to you, "Hey, did you hear? There's this girl named Mary in the Hospital downtown, and she had a baby the other day, and they say she'd never had sex with anyone!" By itself, this would be kind of cool news, and (assuming you believed me), you might tell a friend or two, and perhaps the story would spread for a week or so. But then it would die out. It's a moderately interesting meme, but in today's world where supermarket tabloid headlines shout impossible "facts" daily, it wouldn't be long before this "Virgin Mary" meme faded into oblivion.

But the Christian version of this meme is coupled with thousands of other Christian memes, including memes such as: There is one God; Jesus Christ was God's son; You are inherently sinful, but accepting Christ can absolve you; If you accept Christ, you will be magnificently rewarded; if you don't accept Christ, you will be horribly punished; The Bible is God's inerrant word; You should convert non-Christians to Christianity; There are priests who know more than you about God, Christ and the Bible ... and many, many more.

These Christian memes are an example of a *memeplex,* a set of mutually dependent, symbiotic memes, each one of which probably would not survive, but when taken as a group, become a *survivor*, a set of concepts that are passed reliably and frequently from one brain to the next. Religion is an example of an especially rich and powerful memeplex.

Notice the symbiosis in the Christian memeplex: The individual memes each benefit from the complex, and contribute to the survival

of other memes in the complex. The relationship is mutually beneficial. These memes together form a very powerful memeplex that has
survived for nearly two thousand years.

This book is also a large memeplex. Each chapter, and each section within each chapter, introduces you to new memes. Any one
topic, like the *Martyrdom* meme, is interesting, but hardly likely to
change your fundamental views on religion. But taken together, the
memeplex presented in this book is far more powerful (or so the
author hopes!) than the sum of the individual memes.

Religion as Memes

*Ignorance more frequently begets confidence than does
knowledge: it is those who know little, and not those who
know much, who so positively assert that this or that
problem will never be solved by science.*
– Charles Darwin

Earlier, we studied the nine great trends in religion memes,
things like intolerance, polytheism-to-monotheism, and globalization. Now that we've defined memes more clearly, and had a quick
lesson on Evolution Science, let's make sure we understand that religion is a huge, magnificent memeplex.

Most societies spend vast amounts of time and effort passing
their religious beliefs to their children. It ranks at the top of things
our parents expect us to learn, alongside reading, writing, arithmetic,
history, and science. In fact, some parents (particularly those in
America's more conservative churches) consider their children's religious training to be the only truly important subject; reading is of
course necessary so that one can study the scriptures, but arithmetic,
critical thinking, and particularly science, are often far down the list
of priorities for these parents. Tiny children who have just learned
their first words are sent to Sunday School every week to begin
learning the memes. Kindergarteners act in Christmas plays about
the birth of Jesus. Muslims teach their boys to show their devotion
by praying five times every day. For many families, visiting their

place of worship on the Sabbath (which falls on Friday, Saturday or Sunday, depending on your faith) is mandatory.

This is the hallmark of cultural evolution, of a memplex: It is information that is passed, very deliberately, very reliably, and with high fidelity, from one person to the next, from parent to child, from generation to generation.

Religion is the all-time best self-replicating meme complex in the history of humans.

The Danger of the Metaphor

The folly of mistaking a paradox for a discovery, a metaphor for a proof, a torrent of verbiage for a spring of capital truths, and oneself for an oracle, is inborn in us.
– Paul Vale'ry (1871-1945)

Years ago, in my electrical engineering days, I was working late one night trying to debug a circuit I'd designed and built. Things were going pretty well, until all at once the circuit went completely dead. No matter where I put my oscilloscope's probe or my volt-meter, nothing. Nada. Zilch. I checked the power supply – plenty of voltage. The oscilloscope itself? Still working. The voltmeter? As accurate as ever. The circuit? Still dead.

Then I realized, to my chagrin, that I'd been putting the oscillo-scope and voltmeter on my *blueprints*, not on the circuit itself! I was so used to thinking of the circuitry in the abstract "language" of an electrical engineer's circuit diagram, that the two blended together in my mind. No doubt the lateness of the hour contributed. The great philosopher and mathematician René Descartes (from whose name we get our word, *cartography*, the science of map making), once said, "Don't confuse the map with the terrain." In other words, the map is just a *model* of reality, not reality itself. My late-night mis-take was exactly that: I confused the map itself (the circuit's blue-print) for the terrain (the circuit).

The same thing can happen when discussing evolution. We use many words in a metaphorical sense, and build a "mental model" of the process of natural selection that includes many verbs and adjectives drawn from everyday life. For example, we say "the Yahweh meme mutated..." which suggests some kind of active, intentional motivation from the meme. Or we say, "Each species wants to survive," or "Competition is fierce between memes." It is important to remember that these are just metaphors. There is no desire, intentionality, motivation or any other emotion in the process of evolution. Natural selection, whether for creatures or for memes, is nothing more than a filtering process.

We use a strainer to remove the tea leaves from our tea, and we might say, "The strainer lets the tea through and stops the leaves," suggesting that the strainer somehow has an active part to play in the process. But we all know that it is a metaphor, that filtering tea is a purely mechanical process. When we say, "The tea strainer lets the tea through," it is an entirely different meaning than when we say, "The policeman lets the pedestrians through."

Darwin himself wrote about this very problem in *Origin of the Species*. Darwin noted that for brevity and convenience, we use words which have other connotations, and must be careful not to read too much into these terms:

> *[Some] have objected that the term* selection *implies conscious choice in the animals which become modified; and it had even been urged that, as plants have no volition, natural selection is not applicable to them! In the literal sense of the word, no doubt, natural selection is a false term; ... It has been said that I speak of natural selection as an active power or Deity; but who objects to an author speaking of the attraction of gravity as ruling the movements of the planets? Every one knows what is meant and is implied by such metaphorical expressions; and they are almost necessary for brevity. So again it is difficult to avoid personifying the word Nature; but I mean by Nature, only the aggregate action and product of many natural laws, and by laws [I*

mean] the sequence of events as ascertained by us. With a little familiarity such superficial objections will be forgotten.

As we continue our discussion of memes and evolution, keep in mind that the words we use are metaphorical, and that evolution is an entirely inanimate process.

An Example: Was Joseph Jesus' Father or Not?

If anyone comes to me and does not hate his father and mother, his wife and children, his brothers and sisters, yes, even his own life, he cannot be my disciple.
– Jesus Christ (Luke 14:26)

The battle over *adoptionism* during the second century AD is an example of competing memes responding to evolutionary pressure. The *adoptionist meme* says that Jesus was born human, not divine and later *adopted* by Yahweh as His son. Adoptionists believed that Joseph was Jesus' father and Mary was his mother (*not* a virgin), and that through Jesus' sinless devotion, God was very pleased and took Jesus as His own son, *making* him divine at Jesus' death. The *anti-adoptionist meme* is the now-familiar (i.e. orthodox) view, that Jesus was born of a virgin and was divine from birth, and that Jesus and God are part of a single Holy Trinity.

The scribes of the second century were educated men, well aware of the debate that was raging about this question. Some of the gospels they were copying contained phrases that supported the Adoptionist's beliefs. When Joseph and Mary took Jesus to the Temple, and the holy man Simon blessed Jesus, "his father and mother were marveling at what was said to him" (Luke 2:33). The scribes changed this to "Joseph and his mother..." In several other places, Jesus' original "parents" were changed to "Joseph and his mother".

With the Council of Nicaea, the anti-adoptionist meme won the day. The subtle alterations of the Gospel helped its case by changing the meme-environment slightly in its favor. The adoptionist meme had several revivals through the centuries, but these were quickly suppressed by the anti-adoptionist meme, which by then was firmly entrenched as Christian orthodoxy.

Summary: Evolution and Memes

It may be that our role on this planet is not to worship God, but to create him.
– Arthur C. Clarke

This chapter has been somewhat of a whirlwind tour of the principles of evolution, and how they can be "abstracted" and applied to memes. Let's take a quick look back:

Reproduction is the first principle of evolution. While the "reproductive motive" for biological life ranges from simple biochemistry to complex mating rituals, whatever the motive force may be, it is encoded in the genes. Similarly, memes have a wide variety of motivating features that cause you to repeat them, to teach them to someone else, but it is the meme itself that contains this motive force, that has the impetus for its own reproduction.

Overpopulation, the tendency of all species to produce far more offspring than can survive in each generation, provides the raw material for *natural selection,* the process that weeds out the less fit, and passes on the more fit individuals. Memes, like biological life, have these same two features: There are far more ideas generated than can survive, and only the best ones get passed on to the next generation.

And finally, *mutation* is the source of all variability, the origin of all change and improvement in species. Although mutation is random and mostly detrimental, occasionally a beneficial mutation occurs, which is rapidly amplified in the population by *natural selection.* Memes, like genes, are subject to mutation, but they additionally can be modified deliberately, with intent.

We also noted that memes, like genes, can be confined to a ecological *niche*, a particular subset of the whole ecology that is suitable to the meme's "needs."

In other words, both genes and memes are subject to the fundamental principles of evolution. Both consist of self-replicating information that tends to overpopulate, both are subject to change and mutation, and both are filtered by natural selection. The result is the creation of increasingly complex, intertwined entities: genomes for DNA, and memeplexes for ideas.

Interlude: The Southern Baptists

I never told my religion nor scrutinized that of another. I never attempted to make a convert nor wished to change another's creed. I have judged of others' religion by their lives, for it is from our lives and not from our words that our religion must be read. By the same test must the world judge me.
– Thomas Jefferson

I had the opportunity to become deeply involved for several years with a family that attended the Church of Christ. For those not familiar with America's churches, the Church of Christ is considered conservative even by the mainstream Southern Baptists. This is quite something, because the Southern Baptists are considered very conservative by almost all other churches.

The heads of this family, whom I will call Ruth and William (not their real names) were from a small town in the heart of America's "Bible Belt." I liked both Ruth and William, Ruth in particular, because unlike so many of the others in her church, she liked to talk about religion, and was willing to answer my questions.

Not long after I met Ruth, I couldn't resist prodding her a bit. "Ruth," I asked, "there's something I just don't understand. The Church of Christ says I'm going to Hell, to endure never ending torture and pain. But Ruth, I'm a good man. I go to work, I'm raising three children, I'm honest, and I serve my community. In short, I do everything the Church of Christ says I should do, except belong to the Church. How can it be that God can condemn a good man like me to such horrors, just because I don't accept your particular interpretation of the Bible?"

This really put Ruth on the spot. Like many Southern Baptists, Ruth was taught many things that just seemed wrong to her. But the Baptist culture has an almost irresistible force to conformity, and those who question the Church of Christ's interpretation of the Bible are immediately and severely chastised by the community. Yet ... here I was, someone she could talk to honestly without fear.

Ruth thought about this for a minute. Finally, she told me in a quiet voice, "Well, you'll be judged by your beliefs, and I'll be judged by mine."

I thought this was a remarkable opinion from a woman who was a born-and-bred Southern Baptist, went to church every Sunday of her life, and had never studied any religion or philosophy outside of the teachings of the Church of Christ.

But I was saddened a few year later when I discovered that Ruth and William thought they were going to Hell, in spite of living virtuous lives. The reason? Their adult children had rejected the Church of Christ, so according to the Southern Baptist Church, Christ considered Ruth and William to be mortal sinners, not deserving of God's glory. They, like me, are apparently headed for the eternal fires and cruel torture of Hell, for the sin of raising their children to be open-minded and inquisitive.

4. Religion Grows Up

Reprise: Abraham to Jesus

Nothing shocks me more in the men of religion and their flocks than their pretensions to be the only religious people.
– Jean Guehenno

By the time Jesus was born, polytheism was still widespread, but monotheism had a solid stronghold among the Jews. In spite of being a minority view, the Yahweh meme had *evolved* all of the critical features that made Yahweh into a viable monotheistic deity. Let us do a quick review:

- Yahweh was no longer a specialist god of war. Now he could answer all prayers.
- Instead of merely demanding loyalty, he now claimed to be the *only* god. He had shed his jealousy of other gods, and instead simply denied that they existed. Yahweh claimed to be the only god, a much more sophisticated meme than mere jealousy.
- He began to actively *destroy* other religions. He told the Jews it was OK to torture and kill non-believers and vandalize or destroy their temples. Violence against other religions was a virtue, not a sin.
- He shed his regional association, and could be worshipped anywhere.
- He had changed from an earthly corporeal god who could sit down to dinner with Abraham, to a ethereal, overpowering figure whose very presence would overwhelm a human.
- He was no longer subject to the moral judgement of mere humans through natural philosophy and logic, and instead was transformed into the fundamental source of all morality. His decisions and actions could no longer be questioned.

- He had shed his bully image and was now a kind, altruistic, loving god.
- He had become asexual and above human temptations.

With these memes in place, the Yahweh meme was poised to take over Western civilization.

The Intolerance Meme Grows Up

The best political weapon is the weapon of terror. Cruelty commands respect. Men may hate us. But, we don't ask for their love; only for their fear.
– Heinrich Himmler (1900-1945)

We've already claimed that the genesis of the *Intolerance* meme was one of the most important ideas in the history of the world. The murder and destruction justified by King Josiah in the name of Yahweh (*2 Chronicles*) was bad, but Josiah's intolerance pales by comparison to the acts of intolerance that followed in the next two millennia.

Ironically, the *Intolerance* meme's next big moment in history worked against the Christians: The Christians' monotheism offended the Romans. Recall that Jews and Christians refused to acknowledge or pay homage to other gods. This really irked the Romans, because they equated this with disrespect to the empire. Nero, who was probably crazy, took advantage of the widespread dislike of Christians by blaming them for the great fire (64 AD) that destroyed most of Rome, a fire he may have set himself. Nero diverted suspicion by accusing the Christians, which triggered the first wave of murder and torture of Christians.

The systematic persecutions of Christians began with Maximin in the second century, and continued for the next 150 years. Christians were burned, crucified, fed to lions, wrapped in fresh hides to be torn apart by ravenous dogs ... all of the horrid and cruel methods the Romans could think of. The last and most extensive of these persecutions was the war on monotheism itself, waged by Diocletian and Galerius near the beginning of the fourth century.

But in spite of this long and sad chapter in Roman history, the ultimate irony is that more Christians were killed by *other Christians* after the Roman persecution stopped. In 313 AD, Galerius decriminalized Christianity, and two years later, the Emperors Constantine I and Licineus issued the Edict of Milan, which went even further, declaring that the Empire was neutral with respect to religion. This may have seemed like a good thing to the Christians, but it turned out to be a disaster. Anyone could worship any god, and a Christian could join any of the hundreds of Christian sects that had sprung up since the death of Jesus. Christian "orthodoxy" (literally, "right thought") was taking root, and Christians were well acquainted with the *Intolerance* meme from their Jewish heritage They began to persecute and kill one another in record numbers, just for believing the wrong version of Christianity. In the century that followed the Edict of Milan, more Christians died at the hands of other Christians than the Romans killed in a century and a half of persecutions.

The *Intolerance* meme continued its work down through the centuries. The Crusades saw wanton massacres of "pagans" by Christians, beginning with the First Crusade, in which the entire population of Jerusalem was murdered, man, woman and child:

"No one ever saw or heard of such slaughter of pagan people, for funeral pyres were formed from them like pyramids, and no one knows their number except God alone."
– Gesta Francorum ("The Deeds of the Franks"), a Latin chronicle of the First Crusade, around 1100 AD, anonymous.

The Christians justified these holy wars against Jews and Muslims by taking a chapter from the Jew's history: They claimed they were "God's New Chosen People."

On top of the outright wars, torture and murder in the name of Yahweh, there was also the suppression of "heretical" knowledge. The most famous case is the trial, conviction, and incarceration (commuted to house arrest) of Galileo Galilei by the Roman Catholic Church for contradicting the account of Genesis in the Bible, when he demonstrated that the Earth orbits around the Sun. This tradition, the suppression of knowledge and inquiry, continues full strength even today, with modern Creationists from America's ultra-conservative churches, who try to prevent the teaching of science (evolution in particular) in America's schools. Knowledge and truth are the enemy of the *Intolerance* meme, and it has adapted religious and political methods to fight back.

Some of the largest migrations of humans in history were justified by the *Intolerance* meme. American schoolchildren know King Ferdinand and Queen Isabella, the Catholic Monarchs of Spain, as forward-thinking visionaries who funded Columbus in his "discovery" of America. But American History schoolbooks often, when telling the story of Columbus, omit the fact that Isabella and Ferdinand also presided over the Spanish Inquisition, and omit the fact that in that same year, 1492, Ferdinand and Isabella drove all of the Jews out of Spain, confiscated all their worldly possessions (mostly because many Jews were wealthy and the Monarchy was broke), and forced them to flee in complete destitution. One of the few countries to offer refuge to the Jews was the Ottoman Empire. In some ways, the Jews were lucky – they avoided the Spanish Inquisition, which prosecuted approximately 150,000 Christians, of whom about 3,000 to 5,000 were actually executed.

The early history of America is largely a result of the *Intolerance* meme. The Puritans were a persecuted Christian minority in England, at odds with the "official" Christian Church of England doctrine, so they fled to America to establish their own Puritan town. Ironically, the Puritans, and other groups that followed, in spite of being victims of persecution, were no more tolerant than their former persecutors – once they arrived on the shores of America, they were quick to impose their own version of Christianity on everyone in sight.

Historically, the Muslims were more often the victims of Christian intolerance than the perpetrators. In fact, the period of Moorish rule in Iberia prior to the Catholic takeover, was a Golden Age of tolerance. Muslims, Jews and Christians all lived side by side, worshipped in freedom, learned about one another's culture and religion, and engaged in deep and thoughtful discourse. The intercourse between cultures resulted in fantastic advances in many areas, including mathematics, philosophy, and theology. But that Golden Age of Tolerance died out with the rise and dominance of the Catholic Church in the region.

In spite of their early tolerance, some groups that claim to be Muslim have picked up the *Intolerance* meme, just like their Christian and Jewish predecessors, and they've learned it all too well. Modern events, such as the destruction of Buddhist shrines in Afghanistan by the Taliban government, and the civil war between the Shi'ite and Sunni Muslims in Iraq following the destruction of the Iraqi government by American forces, show that the Muslims are perfectly capable of incorporating the *Intolerance* meme into their theology, in spite of the teachings of Mohammad, who taught that all faiths should be respected equally.

A full accounting of the tragedies justified by the *Intolerance* meme would fill thousands and thousands of books. Murder, torture, poverty, wars by the dozens and hundreds, forced migrations ... the list of atrocities is appalling.

When discussing these acts of murder, torture, etc., it is difficult to know whether they were *caused* by religious intolerance, or merely justified after the fact. For example, Isabella and Ferdinand might have conducted something like the Spanish Inquisition even without the Church's backing. The underlying motive was power and wealth, and they may have used Catholicism as a cover-up for crimes they would have committed anyway. Stalin's reign of terror makes Ferdinand and Isabella look like amateurs, and Stalin was an atheist.

Some acts of intolerance are plainly in support of the Religion Virus, such as the suppression of Galileo's discovery that the Earth isn't the center of the universe. Such knowledge threatened both the orthodox view, as well as the authority of the Roman Catholic Church. After all, if they were wrong about a geocentric universe, what else might be challenged? But generally speaking, it is difficult or impossible to separate cause and effect. Because of this, I am careful to use the word "justified" when talking about the *Intolerance* meme. It may be that "caused" is a more correct term in some cases, but we can't know.

Before we leave this topic, it is important to remind ourselves *why* such a negative meme could become integrated into the memeplex of the world's great religions. The "Golden Age of Tolerance" in Iberia under the Moors illustrates the brutal truth about the *Intolerance* meme. Which religion dominates Spain and Portugal today? The Roman Catholic Church. It was the religion that (in the 1400s) had the most well-developed *Intolerance* meme. The Moors let Jews and Christians worship right alongside the Muslims. Although that may seem like a wise, enlightened and moral way to run a country, it doesn't spread Islam. By contrast, when the Catholics took over, with their strong *Intolerance* meme, they wiped out the other religions.

It doesn't matter whether Isabella and Ferdinand were right or wrong, moral or immoral, or whether the *Intolerance* meme caused or merely justified their actions. All that matters is that the Roman Catholic Church gained, and Islam and Judaism lost. The Roman Catholics memeplex became more numerous, the Judaism and Islamic memeplexes became fewer. Catholicism had more parishioners, the Jews and Muslims were killed or fled, along with the memes for Judaism and Islam. The Muslim's "tolerance meme" wasn't a survivor, so it died out, whereas the Catholic's *Intolerance* meme was taught to the next generation, because it survived.

This is *survival of the fittest* at its simplest and best. The Spanish Inquisition was a terrible, immoral tragedy, but from an evolutionary point of view, it was a success.

St. Paul expands the Globalization Meme

The Bible is not my book, and Christianity is not my reli-
gion. I could never give assent to the long, complicated
statements of Christian dogma.
– Abraham Lincoln (1809-1865)

In addition to his preaching and letters, St. Paul started one of
the most crucial ideas to the spread of the Christian religion: Paul
argued that the teachings of Jesus, and the power of Yahweh, should
be shared with the *goyim*, not just the Jews. This was a radical
departure from Jewish tradition, and offended the other disciples of
Jesus who believed that Jesus' teachings were just for the Jews,
God's chosen people:

Then Paul and Barnabas answered them boldly: "We had to
speak the word of God to you first. Since you reject it and do
not consider yourselves worthy of eternal life, we now turn
to the Gentiles."
– Acts 13:46

In our chapter on *Religion's Infancy*, we studied the *Globaliza-*
tion meme, which converted Yahweh from a regional god of war,
into a global god whom the Jews could worship anywhere in the
world. This was a critical mutation for the Yahweh memeplex,
because it allowed Judaism to break out of its ancestral homeland.
But although Yahweh had become geographically global, he was
still ethnically local – only the Jews were his "Chosen People," so
there was no reason to convince non-Jews to worship Yahweh.
Yahweh was "stuck in a rut," with a limited audience.

The Apostle Paul changed that. Saint Paul was a Jew and a
Roman citizen who studied under the well-known Rabbi Gamaliel,
and was engaged in the persecution of Christians. He was headed to
Damascus, apparently to eradicate a Christian community, when he
had a blinding vision of Jesus and was converted to Christianity,
becoming one of the most important preachers in Christianity's history. In addition to his preaching, Paul was a literate man and wrote

many letters to Christians, answering their questions and correcting their misunderstandings, letters which are now one of the most important parts of the New Testament of the Christian Bible.

> *Understand, then, that those who believe are children of Abraham. The Scripture foresaw that God would justify the Gentiles by faith, and announced the gospel in advance to Abraham: "All nations will be blessed through you." So those who have faith are blessed along with Abraham, the man of faith.*
> *– Galatians 3:7-9*

The *Globalization* meme, which previously had expanded the worship of Yahweh worldwide, had once again mutated, this time allowing it to spread outside of the Jewish people. Yahweh (the Christian version, that is) became a truly universal god-memeplex, a god who could be worshipped anywhere, by anyone.

The benefits of this mutation of the Yahweh memeplex (that is, the Christian version of the Yahweh memeplex) are obvious: The Christian version of the Yahweh meme is worshipped by far more people than the Jewish version. Its *ecological niche* (the "place" where the meme can survive – a topic we will study at length in the next chapter) was vastly expanded by this mutation.

The Guilt Meme

> *A woman should learn in quietness and full submission. I do not permit a woman to teach or to have authority over a man; she must be silent. For Adam was formed first, then Eve. And Adam was not the one deceived; it was the woman who was deceived and became a sinner.*
> *1 Timothy 2:11-14*

Many cultures have a much more open and casual attitude towards pleasures such as sex, wine and leisure than Western civilization. For example, some Polynesian cultures allowed teenagers to engage in sex freely. Ancient Egyptian language appears to have no word for "virgin," as virginity was not an important concept. Pre-Christian pagan religions throughout the Roman Empire considered sex to be an essential part of their worship, honoring the fertility and pleasures that the gods had bestowed; ritual sex was common, and often an essential part of worship.

The Christians who first arrived in the South Seas may have thought Polynesians were utterly without morals, but they were mistaken. The Polynesians had strong moral codes, and (for example) were expected to be monogamous once married; sexual freedom was only the prerogative of teenagers.

The Jews believe that sex and marriage are holy and divine. Rabbis are expected to marry, to have a respectful and happy sex life with their wives, become fathers, and set an example for other men and women in the community. The Jews of Jesus' time believed that it was sinful to *avoid* pleasures like sex and wine. God did *not* want humans to suffer, nor was suffering the way to find God. Rather, God had made pleasures for humans to enjoy. To avoid these pleasures was to deny God's gifts.

To the Jews, the idea of inherited sin is abhorrent, and against the word of Yahweh as taught in Deuteronomy:

Fathers shall not be put to death for their children, nor children put to death for their fathers; each is to die for his own sin.
– Deuteronomy 24:16

The Greeks, especially Plato, Socrates and Aristotle, formulated a rational approach to ethics (discussed briefly in the *Godly Origin of Morals* section earlier) that had a profound influence on the world. Aristotle's *Nicomachean Ethics* (350 BC) is the most complete and well-known work describing Greek Ethics, and is a towering intellectual achievement. Reading it, one wonders how, over two thousand years later, we haven't come close to the inherently moral standards laid down by the Greeks.

The Christians, in the guise of Tertullian of Carthage, followed by Saint Augustine, turned the natural morality of pagan societies, and the Rational Ethics of the Greeks, on its head. The *Guilt* meme began with the vilification of all natural human pleasures and desires, sex in particular. Tertullian created the term *original sin*, the idea that we inherit sin from Adam and Eve's transgressions, but Tertullian's influence was limited because of his truly extreme views. But Augustine, who became a Catholic bishop, picked up Tertullian's idea of original sin, and turned it into a powerful meme.

Augustine's revulsion with his own sexuality can be seen in his explanation of the male erection. Instead of considering it a healthy, natural reaction that a man experiences upon seeing a desirable woman, Augustine decided that the male erection was the flesh revolting against God's will. That is, the human soul naturally wants to be chaste (why? Augustine doesn't say), but the flesh revolts into sin, and is disgusting. Augustine carried this revulsion of sex to an extreme: All sex of any sort outside of marriage was sinful, and even within marriage sex was regrettable, and was only permitted for the procreation of children. This is particularly ironic given Augustine's ten-year relationship with his true love, a common country girl, who bore him his son, but whom he was forced to abandon when his mother insisted on a society marriage. Some argue that the heartbroken Augustine's deep anguish over this lost love may have caused him to reject love and sex; that as a *post-facto* justification for his loss, Augustine formulated his anti-sex philosophy that became entrenched in Christianity.

Augustine also laid down the theological foundation for reviling women, by arguing that Eve's transgression was of such a magnitude that one's own death couldn't pay for it. This leads to the conclusion that women are responsible for all evil in the world, and in particular for the need for Jesus to die a horrible death by crucifixion. That's quite a transgression, for an entire gender to be responsible for the torture and death of Jesus.

Virtually all other religions find the views of the Roman Catholic Church, and its derivative churches, regarding original sin and the vilification of women to be peculiar at best, and outrageous at worst. Even the Eastern Christian Churches, which grew out of the split and subsequent fall of the Roman Empire, consider their

Western brethren's doctrine of original sin to be wrong. But Augustine was declared a saint, and his philosophy is at the very core of the Roman Catholic Church and most of the spin-offs that make up the bulk of American and European Christian churches.

The Catholic Church's official position is that Augustine combined Aristotle's teachings on morality with Christian theology, producing a more ethical church. But the opposite is true: Augustine corrupted the very foundation of Aristotle's ethics. Aristotelian ethics works *towards* natural human desires and pleasures, but Christian ethics tend to turn people *away* from pleasure and toward asceticism and abstinence.

Here, we must be very careful not to paint all Christian churches with a single brush. There are vast differences between various denominations' interpretation of the Bible's teachings. For example, Roman Catholics enjoy wine, beer and strong drink in moderation, following Aristotle's ethics, and the Roman Catholic Church has sponsored some of the finest musicians and composers in the history of the world. By contrast the Church of Christ, one of America's conservative Baptist denominations, believe that alcohol is sinful, they don't allow musical instruments (only vocal music) in their worship, and they frown on dancing.

Using Aristotle's ethics, people went happily about the business of enjoying themselves, in moderation, whether it was through sex, wine, food, song, games, pride in their work, or rest on their days off. Consider Aristotle's view of leisure:

And happiness is thought to depend on leisure; for we are busy that we may have leisure, and make war that we may live in peace.
– Aristotle, Nicomachean Ethics, Book X, Chapter 7

But Augustine changed all that: Now anything pleasurable was a vice. The Christians instead declared leisure (sloth) to be one of the seven deadly sins. Or take lust: Christian theology teaches that *chastity* is the opposite of *lust*, and chastity is a *virtue*. This is the exact opposite of Aristotle's view, which is that *both* lust and chastity are bad, and that sex should be practiced with healthy moderation.

The Christians' "seven deadly sins," lust, hunger, a desire for leisure, anger, envy and pride, pretty much sum up human nature. We all feel these things. By turning our natural, instinctive emotions into sins, the Christians achieved what the Jews (and others) had failed to achieve in two thousand years: They made people feel bad for following their human nature.

Augustine's philosophy of guilt was brilliant. Before Augustine, a decent, moral person could live and exemplary life, never commit a crime, never hurt anyone, marry and raise a fine family, and at the end of life, be in the good graces of Yahweh for eternity. But Augustine ended that; merely being good and moral isn't enough. You *had* to accept Christianity or face grave consequences.

The Heaven and Hell Memes

Maybe this world is another planet's hell.
– Aldous Huxley (1894-1963)

The concept of an afterlife is ancient. One of the oldest questions in the world is, "Is there life after death?" Philosophers ask the same question a different way: "Is the corporeal body separate from the soul?" In other words, is there some essential part of us, called the "self" or "soul" or "conscious entity," something that inhabits the body while the body is alive, but that carries on, perhaps to some final destination, or perhaps to be reincarnated in a different body?

The earlier concepts of the afterlife, such as the early Greek *Hades* and the Jewish *Sheol,* tend to picture a dark and featureless, somewhat gloomy afterlife. It's not unpleasant in the sense of punishment, more like a place where the soul either sleeps or wanders after death. Early Greek, Roman and Jewish religions didn't distinguish Heaven and Hell – everyone went to the same place. The Greek Hades is perhaps the best known to Westerners since the term is still in widespread use, and studied as part of World History. The Jewish *Sheol* was originally very much like Hades, although it didn't have the full cast of characters of Greek Mythology.

As time went by, the Jews, Greeks and Romans divided their afterlife according to the virtues of its inhabitants. Hades was divided into sections that include the *Elysian Fields* where the heroic and valorous spent eternity, and *Tarterus*, where for example, Sisyphus had to spend eternity rolling a boulder up a hill only to have it slip and roll back down, time and again. By the time of Jesus, the Jews had planted the seeds of our modern Heaven and Hell. They still believed that all souls went to the same place, *Sheol,* to await the resurrection, but additionally, the good waited happily, whereas bad people were punished. The parable of Lazarus and Dives, recounted in the gospel of Luke in the New Testament, illustrated what many Jews of the time believed, that a good man (Lazarus the beggar) would spend eternity in the happy company of Abraham, and the bad man (David the rich man) spent eternity in torment.

The Christians were the ones who "turned up the volume" on the ideas of Heaven and Hell. Dante's *The Divine Comedy*, written in the early fourteenth century, describes Hell, Purgatory and Paradise in vivid and horrifying details. It is considered an encapsulation of the Heaven-Purgatory-Hell meme's evolution during the Middle Ages leading up to the Renaissance. Dante put to pen to paper, and created a vivid, thoroughly detailed, and well-crafted version of what many believed in his time. One can see the Greek, Judaic and Pagan influences in the Christian view of Heaven, Purgatory and Hell, but by Dante's time, the Christians had refined and polished it beyond anything that had come before.

The Christian afterlife had several important additions over its predecessors.

First, the rewards and punishments were dramatically amplified over the Judaic *Sheol* and Pagan *Hades* traditions. The Christian *Heaven* meme evolved into a place where you enjoy absolute and unconditional bliss, and the Christian *Hell* meme evolved to a place where you suffer unimaginable pain and torture.

Second, in the Christian (and some Jewish) versions of the *Heaven/Hell* memes, you only get one chance. There is no reincarnation; if you screw up, you're punished forever, and if you are good, you're happy forever. This closed a "loophole" in the afterlife, one that allowed believers to say, "Well, if I screw up this time, the worst is that I'll be sent back to try again." No more second chances.

Third, the Christian rewards or punishment, embodied in the *Heaven/Hell* memes became badly out of line with the deeds. Eternal torture in Hell was like murdering a child for spilling milk. The rewards of Heaven are similarly out of line – a good life on Earth gains you unending bliss, not in proportion to your deeds on earth, not for a lifetime, or a thousand, or a million years, but *forever*.

The Proselytism Meme

Then Jesus came to them and said, "All authority in heaven and on earth has been given to me. Therefore go and make disciples of all nations, baptizing them in the name of the Father and of the Son and of the Holy Spirit, and teaching them to obey everything I have commanded you."
– Matthew 28:18-20

The common cold is a virus that lives in the fluids of your nose and throat, and it's fairly fragile. Expose it to a dry, cool environment, and it's dead. And if it stays in your body too long, it's dead – your body develops antibodies within a week or two of infection. So the cold virus has a problem: It has to infect someone else quickly or die. The cold virus achieves by making you sneeze and cough. A sneeze or cough ejects a lot of saliva and mucous in the form of tiny droplets, and the cold virus hitches a ride in these nice little "microclimates" to its next victim.

We see this sort of "amplified distribution" throughout nature – many, many species have amazing and clever ways to spread their offspring. Every kid who lives near a maple tree knows that it has "helicopter seeds" that spin like little propellers, and can be carried long distances by the wind. The maple tree, like the cold virus, is spreading itself wider. Fruit trees wrap their seeds first in a tough coating that can survive through the gut, then in a tasty flesh that is good to eat, prompting animals to ingest their seed along with the tasty fruit, and later defecate it a long distance from the parent tree.

Religious proselytizing is very much like the sneeze that the virus induces: It forcibly propagates the religious memeplex into places it otherwise would not have access to. Without proselytizing, each religion would only spread by "intimate contact," a potential convert who of his/her own choice decided to learn about and adopt it. In a nutshell, it is "passive spread" versus "active spread." Kissing is passive: the virus doesn't contribute to its own spread. Sneezing is active: The viral infection itself triggers the mechanism for its own propagation. The *Proselytism* meme is a form of active spreading, because it "takes God's message to the uninitiated."

A number of religions do *not* advocate proselytism. Judaism avoids it, some say largely because of the historical dominance of Christianity and Islam, and the fear of inciting further persecution. Hinduism teaches that there is but one faith, but it is revealed differently to different peoples, so the idea of converting someone from one faith to another doesn't really make sense, although there are sects, such as the Hare Krishnas, who do proselytize.

Does proselytizing work? Let's compare the spread of the non-proselytizing religions with those that do proselytize. The Church of Jesus Christ of Latter Day Saints (the LDS Church, or Mormons) are well known for the "missions" that are required of all young men and some young women in the LDS Church. And the results are dramatic. According to the American Council of Churches, the LDS Church was the second-fastest growing church in American in 2006. Which church beat it? The Assemblies of God, the other church with an avowed goal to have mission and growth in "every country in the world." In 2006, a year in which seventeen of the twenty largest churches in America reported no growth or *lost* membership, the LDS Church grew by 1.74% and the Assemblies of God grew 1.81%. The only other major church that grew at all was the Catholic church, at 0.83%. This might seem like decent growth for the Catholics, until you realize that the population of the United States grew faster than the Catholic Church (0.89% that same year). So the Catholics are losing ground too! Only the most aggressive two churches in America, the ones with the strongest *Proselytism* meme, actually gained ground.

(*Note:* The American Council of Churches also reported that the top-growing church was the Orthodox Church in America, however, the numbers were highly suspect, and some reports put their membership at ten percent of their reported value, with negative growth. I have therefore put them on the "no growth or declining" list, which may or may not be correct.)

The *Proselytism* meme is interesting because it shows us evolution in action. Churches that actively proselytize are growing, all the others are static or shrinking. At a growth rate of 1.81%, the Assemblies of God church will double its membership every thirty-eight years. By contrast, many of the other Christian churches in America are *shrinking* at that same rate or more, meaning their memberships will drop by fifty percent every few decades. It doesn't take the gift of prophecy to see that in a few hundred years, the Assemblies of God and LDS churches will dominate in America.

The Armageddon Meme

Science never cheered up anyone. The truth about the human situation is just too awful.
-- Kurt Vonnegut, Timequake

The quote from Kurt Vonnegut above summarizes one of the biggest problems that scientists and atheists have when trying to discuss their understanding of the world with those who believe in God.

Religion has put forth a wonderful idea, that the world under God's guiding hand is essentially a good place. According to this view, Yahweh created a perfect world, one in which there was no evil. But evil forces, represented by Satan and the Serpent of the Garden of Eden (who may be the same, depending on who is telling the story), brought temptation, sin and evil into God's creation. Humankind fell from God's grace, and has been suffering ever since. But all is not lost, the essential goodness of God's universe is still there for all to see, and is exemplified by the good deeds, kindness and redemption seen every day by the faithful. Someday soon, Yahweh will gather His forces and drive the evil out of the world, and the perfection of Yahweh's creation will be restored.

This is a beautiful, and *very* appealing, meme.

On October 3, 2003, the ninth-highest paid celebrities in the United States, two men who together made close to $60 million per year, had their careers utterly destroyed and one of them nearly lost his life. They were never able to return to entertaining, and the hotel where they performed lost over $45 million per year in direct ticket sales, and probably far more in gambling revenues, hotel occupancy and dining. All told, the annual loss must have been in the neighborhood of $75 to $100 million per year. On top of that, over 250 cast and crew members lost their jobs when the show ended, a further loss of income of somewhere around $10 to $20 million per year to them and their families.

That show was, of course, the wonderful *Siegfried and Roy, Masters of the Incredible*, and their famous white tigers at the Mirage Hotel in Las Vegas. The event that caused this financial calamity was that one of the tigers did what tigers do: He bit Roy Horn on the neck, nearly killing him.

Although the facts aren't completely clear, the most reliable witnesses all seem to agree: The tiger, Montecore, wasn't trying to hurt Roy, in fact, quite the opposite. A woman in the front row had a big hairdo that was distracting Montecore, and the woman foolishly reached out to touch the animal. Roy jumped between Montecore and the woman, Montecore took Roy's arm in his teeth, Roy ordered Montecore to "Release!" which he did. Then, tragedy: Roy stepped back, tripped over Montecore's big paws, and fell down. Montecore, by this time afraid and excited, grasped Roy by the neck as he would have a tiger kitten, and dragged him offstage to safety.

Tiger experts (including Siegfried and Roy) say that, had Montecore been attacking Roy, he would have instinctively shaken Roy's body, probably breaking his neck. Instead, he carefully pulled Roy offstage, where stage hands managed to separate the two. Montecore didn't understand that a human doesn't have the same thick, loose skin on the back of his necks that a tiger kitten has, which allows a parent to grasp it safely and carry it around.

Montecore's "gentle" treatment of his friend, Roy Horn, put Roy on the critical list at the hospital for weeks. A portion of Roy's skull had to be removed to relieve the pressure from swelling of his brain. He was transferred to UCLA Medical Center for long-term recovery. Roy Horn eventually regained his speech, but can only walk with assistance.

Although this is not a book about the macabre, nor a horror story, we need to explore this just a bit further to make it absolutely clear. Try to imagine just how horrible Roy Horn's injuries were. Imagine that I asked you to take two or three steak knives from your kitchen, and plunge them into your head and neck. Even one such knife wound would cause you unbearable pain. Then at the same time, I'd like you to put your head in a vice, and crank it down until your skull cracks in several places. This is no joke – it's what happened to Roy Horn. And remember, the tiger wasn't trying to hurt him.

Finally, consider this: This is how a tiger makes its living *every day*. This sort of pain and agony are necessary, not once, not a dozen times, but *thousands* of times in a tiger's lifetime. And not just tigers, but *every* carnivore makes its living this way: Lions, tigers, cheetahs, wolves, coyotes, rattlesnakes, polar bears, killer whales, moray eels, piranhas ... the list goes on and on. The amount of suffering caused by the ordinary day-to-day eating habits of the world's carnivores and parasites is almost beyond human comprehension.

One of the concepts that is hardest for many people to grasp is the utter indifference of nature to suffering. To the deer who is suffering in a tiger's jaws, nothing could matter more. But evolution has no feelings, all that matters is survival. If the tiger's meal causes pain, so it goes. In fact, when a tigress teaches her young to hunt, she will sometimes *deliberately* cause more suffering, by injuring rather than killing her prey, so that her cubs can learn how to properly finish the job. Her survival and that of her cubs shapes her behavior; her prey's suffering does not.

We humans have a bad tendency to anthropomorphize, to assign human feelings and motives to other animals, objects, and events. In this case we'd like imagine that "mother nature" (also known as "evolution") has motives and feelings, that it is malevolent and even evil. Or, some might instead think the tiger himself has evil or cruel intentions. But this is a purely egocentric point of view, "If the tiger is hurting me, it must be cruel." Nothing could be further from the truth. There is no motivation whatsoever to evolution; it just happens. The tiger isn't cruel or evil, it is just following the behavioral patterns that evolution created for its survival. The tiger has no idea about the pain and suffering it causes. Evolution sharpens the tiger's teeth and claws, not to cause pain, but rather to get more food. The pain and suffering are irrelevant side effects from the tiger's evolutionary "point of view."

This is not to say that pain and suffering aren't relevant to evolution; clearly they are. Pain encourages the deer to run faster when the tiger attacks, it keeps us from putting our hands in the fire, or stepping on sharp objects. Pain is a critical trait in evolution, as are happiness, anger, jealousy and all of our emotions. But evolution doesn't "care" about your state of mind, only your survival. If your survival depends on some other creature suffering a painful death, then so it goes. And if some other creature's survival depends on your pain and death, too bad for you. Evolution isn't good or evil, it just favors those who survive.

This is the reality that Kurt Vonnegut is talking about in the quote that starts this section, when he says, "Science never cheered anyone up." The truth about evolution, about suffering, and about the utter indifference of natural selection to our happiness, is really quite unpleasant. Nature is filled with suffering and pain, and the world is *not* a nice place. According to scientists, there is no magical, fun-filled ending: Life is a struggle, and then you die.

Contrast this with the three Abrahamic religions' views of the world. The memes that make up Judaism, Islam and Christianity have, at their core, a loving, perfect Yahweh who is essentially good, and all of our pain and suffering are temporary. Some day, they tell us, this struggle will be over, evil will be driven from the world, and we'll live in peace and harmony.

The contrast between these two memeplexes couldn't be more stark: Evolution's utter indifference, versus Yahweh's absolute benevolence. Is it any wonder that scientists have a hard time getting their memeplex to spread? This is one of the very best examples of survival of the fittest, illustrating that a meme's fitness can be completely divorced from its truthfulness. This truth about nature is so unpleasant that this alone has driven many people away from atheism, back into the reassuring arms of religion.

Synergy: Guilt, Heaven, Hell, and Monotheism

Men have feverishly conceived a heaven only to find it insipid, and a hell to find it ridiculous.
– George Santayana (1863-1952)

To wrap up this chapter, let's take a look at synergy – memes that work together. One of the recurring themes throughout this book is the *memeplex*, a group of mutually supporting memes that together are more than the sum of the parts. The three memes we just studied – Intolerance, Guilt, and Heaven/Hell, plus the Monotheism meme from earlier – are a perfect example of this.

Let's start with a peculiar feature of Monotheism. A polytheist might worship one god over another, but it is purely a practical matter – you pray to a god of love for romance, and a god of war for victory. The idea that you might pick one of the gods and say, "This is the only *real* god, all the others are fakes," doesn't make sense to a polytheist. But the monotheist has made exactly this choice: He has picked one particular god out, and declared that everyone else is wrong. If you could step back 3000 years and forget everything you'd been taught in this modern age, you would probably think the monotheist's beliefs were arrogant and wrong.

Given the monotheist's decision to select just one god above all others, it's not a very big step to select one *church* over all others, and declare that not only is Yahweh the one and only god, but *our particular interpretation of the Bible is the one and the only correct one*. And this leads to the final leap: *You can only get saved by Jesus from your sins by our particular church.* We have the rules, we have the *exclusive* correct interpretation of the scriptures, and any deviation from these rules will result in your eternal damnation in Hell. (Again I remind readers that not all Christian denominations make these claims, but some do.)

Pretty strong stuff, isn't it? This is what you might call a "corollary meme" – let's call it the *Monochurch* meme – the "our church is the only church" meme. Now let's see how this *Monochurch* meme interacts with the others.

The *Intolerance* meme gave religion a huge boost in popularity, because it gave people strong reasons to believe (or pretend to believe) in Yahweh. The *Intolerance* meme was the first *active* weapon that religions used against each other, giving them license to destroy one another's temples and kill one another's members This was a great advance for the Religion Virus memeplex, but like all coercive forces, if it's the only motivation, it leads to reluctant, half-hearted followers.

Next came the *Guilt* meme, which vilified feelings that every healthy human has: sex, hunger, desire, pride, fatigue – pretty much everything good in life was now bad. Previously (for example, under Greek ethics), you had to do something bad in order to feel guilt, but with the Christian's new-found sins, you were guilty simply for being human. On top of that, if you somehow managed to avoid all human temptations and lead an exemplary life, you were *still* guilty, because you inherited Eve's sin! You are in trouble no matter what.

And third, *only Jesus can absolve your sins.* It doesn't matter how sorry you are, it didn't matter how much you do to repent or correct any wrongs you might have done, it doesn't matter what the balance of your good deeds is to your bad deeds. There is only one thing that will save you, and that is to accept the Christian religion's dogma.

And the last "team member" in this memeplex are the *Heaven/Hell* and *Armageddon* memes. If you don't accept the Christian dogma, the consequences are appalling. Eternal damnation and (depending on exactly which branch of Christianity you subscribe to) anything from eternal disappointment to eternal torture.

Going back to where we started, the *Monochurch* meme, we discover that:

- You're guilty no matter what
- Only the Christian church can fix your problem
- If you don't accept the Christian dogma, the punishment is unimaginably severe.

These memes, which mutated and matured to their full power in the Middle Ages, are very powerful indeed when combined. The synergy between them makes the memeplex much more powerful than the mere sum of the memes would suggest.

Interlude: Billy the Racist

Slaves, obey your earthly masters with respect and fear, and with sincerity of heart, just as you would obey Christ. Obey them not only to win their favor when their eye is on you, but like slaves of Christ, doing the will of God from your heart
– Ephesians 6:5-6

In the small town where I grew up, my elementary school had exactly one black student, and just a few kids of Hispanics, Japanese and Chinese ethnicity. Most of the "ethnic diversity" in our town was provided by the Italian fishing community. My parents were liberal Democrats, and worked hard to give their children a deep respect for people of all races, religions and ethnicity. As a college student in the liberal post-Vietnam 1970s, I became even more committed to the liberal cause, and thought that race would simply not be an issue for me.

A decade or so later, a job opportunity took me to live and work in New Orleans for three years. As a born-and-bred California boy, the experience was quite a shock. New Orleans was both amazing and a frightening – in many ways, it is more "third world" than most third-world countries. Magnificent casinos have janitors who never even finished the first grade. Boisterous Mardi Gras parades march past welfare housing projects. Some of the finest musicians in the world play for tips on Bourbon Street, next to drunks passed out on the sidewalks. One night, a close friend of mine who was an emergency-room doctor treated more than thirty *unrelated* gunshot wounds. Some of the public schools were excellent, but at least one school that I visited had broken windows, knee-deep grass, and a student yelling, "Hey, honky, what you doing here?" to the great amusement of his friends. And this was an *elementary* school.

When I purchase my new home in New Orleans, I was quite pleased, perhaps smug, that my middle-class street had five black families and five white families. All of them were quite friendly, and their Southern Hospitality worked its magic, making me and my family feel welcome. I had three school-age children, and before long I was good friends with a number of other families from the school.

My first lesson in personal racism came when I went into a neighborhood supermarket. New Orleans has strong lines of demarcation: One side of a boulevard can be upper-class mansions, and the other side a slum. Apparently, I'd unknowingly crossed one of these lines, from my middle-class, racially mixed neighborhood, into a neighborhood that was exclusively black (and mostly poor) residents. The patrons and employees at the supermarket were just as polite and helpful as could be. The problem was *me*. I was scared. Here I was, for the first time in my life, the only white guy in sight, and it made me *really* nervous. My rational side told me, "These are all just ordinary people, out shopping just like you." But I couldn't help it – deep inside me, I discovered a hidden pool of discomfort with people of a different color. It was a really good experience, one that brought me down off my liberal pedestal into the real world, and prepared me, a little bit at least, for my friend Billy.

One of the wonderful aspects of New Orleans is its diversity. I lived for a decade in the insular world of Silicon Valley. My best friends, to the last one, were engineers. At parties, someone "different" might be an accountant or an attorney. The first time I went to a party in New Orleans, I was amazed to find that among the guests were a tug-boat captain, an oil driller, a geophysicist, a senior editor of the *Times Picayune* newspaper, a couple waiters, a writer, a teacher, and a host of other equally diverse and fascinating people. This group of families would get together every week or two for a big crawfish boil or a barbecue, and enjoy the warm summer evenings and great conversation.

Among these guests was Billy, a tall, thin New Orleans native, the father of a half-dozen or so kids. He made his living as a handyman, doing whatever work came his way. He was a great guy, as nice as could be, always willing to come over and help me if I needed a hand with a project, soft spoken and polite. Although Billy was not well educated, he kept up with politics and current affairs, and he had no trouble holding his own in a debate with the editor of the *Times Picayune*.

My second New Orleans lesson in racism came one day when, in the course of some conversation, Billy confessed that he was an unrepentant racist. I was shocked, not only that my friend Billy held beliefs that I found so objectionable, but also that he was frank and open about it. "I know it's wrong," he said, "but I can't help it. I was raised that way. We were taught that blacks were inferior, and taught to look down on them. I've tried, but I just can't change my ways, I still can't see black folk as equal to whites." Billy at least had the courtesy not to use the "N word," but his confession was a real conundrum for me. If a friend of mine in Silicon Valley had made the same confession, I, and all of my friends, would have ejected him from our social circle. That sort of overt racism is unheard of in California. But in the deep South, racism is still alive and well, and in some circles isn't even shameful.

Then Billy said something that I thought was insightful. "At least I admit it," he said. "Lots of your friends here feel like I do. We were all raised here in the South, and that's what we were taught. These other folks may not want to admit it, but nobody here is colorblind." I thought back to my experience in the grocery store, and how my own latent racism had been there all along, and realized that Billy was right. None of us is without sin. At least Billy was honest about it.

And although I don't approve of his attitude even a little bit, I will say that, when Billy Junior and my son invited a black friend over to play, Billy the elder encouraged them, fixed them lunch, and never once showed any sign of his inner feelings. Billy may have been a racist, but at least he was working hard not to pass it on to Billy Junior and the rest of the his children. He knew his racism was wrong.

Billy understood instinctively that what you're taught as a child is *very* hard to unlearn as an adult. He wasn't able to undo his own biases, but at least he had the courage to be honest, and the strength to not pass his racism on to his own kids.

This story has an interesting epilogue. During my time in New Orleans, I became a big fan of a local Irish band that played every weekend in a pub on Bourbon Street. Sadly, this wonderful old pub was bought by a national restaurant chain, which converted it to a country-western karaoke bar, my worst musical nightmare. But I discovered that the Irish boys were going to be playing at a pub in Metarie, the suburb of New Orleans to the west by the airport.

I arrived at the pub and found a good seat near the band. They launched into their set, but for some reason, I felt very uncomfortable, and started feeling nervous. I couldn't figure out why, the place just seemed very odd and forbidding. Then about half way through the evening, it hit me: Every person in the bar was white. In New Orleans, this was *very* odd, so odd that I immediately realized this was not the bar for me. I'd changed from a man who was nervous in an all-black supermarket, to a man who was uncomfortable in an all-white bar.

It turned out the bar was owned by David Duke, the former head of the racist Ku Klux Klan organization. Blacks knew better than to go in. Racism was still alive and well in New Orleans. I bid my favorite musicians goodbye, and never saw them again.

5. Why Do Humans Talk?

Is Language Adaptive or Accidental?

The word god is for me nothing more than the expression and product of human weaknesses, the Bible a collection of honorable, but still primitive legends which are nevertheless pretty childish. No interpretation no matter how subtle can (for me) change this.
– Albert Einstein

We've talked a lot about *what* memes are, now it's time to ask the question, *Why do memes exist?* This whole book is founded on the concept of memes, and we can't ignore their origin.

Linguists, sociologists and anthropologists have argued for decades over the question, "Why did human language evolve?" Good answers have been proposed, which fall roughly into two camps. The first camp, best represented by the well-known evolution scientists Stephan Jay Gould, holds that human language developed as an accidental side effect of a more powerful brain. Gould's thesis is (very roughly) that increasing intelligence made humans "more fit for survival," and language just came along for the ride.

The second camp argues that human language itself is adaptive, that language made humans more fit for survival. These scientist, well represented by cognitive scientist Steven Pinker, claim that the ability to share knowledge about hunting, food sources, dangers and so forth gave humans a huge evolutionary advantage over their non-speaking competitors, and claim that language evolved specifically as a successful adaptive trait.

But in my view, none of these explanations comes even close to the explanatory power of memetics.

Memes evolved as a new mechanism for evolution. Memes replace genes as the primary adaptive mechanism for humans.

Evolution is Slow

The goal of science is to build better mousetraps. The goal of nature is to build better mice.
– Author Unknown

Consider the principles of Darwin's Evolution Science, and what they imply. For a species to survive, the information in its DNA must meet a number of criteria.

First, the DNA's information must be *very* stable. There are roughly three billion base pairs in the human genome that must be reproduced accurately. That's a *lot* of information. James Michener's semi-historical novel *Hawaii* is over 1000 pages, and a typical page contains about 1000 characters, so Michener's *Hawaii* is roughly one million characters. If the human genome were typed out as characters, it would take 3,000 books the length of *Hawaii* to hold the human genome! Imagine making just one accurate copy of a set of books that takes over 175 meters of space on the bookshelf. Although a certain small error rate is tolerable during reproduction, it is a *very* small rate. If the error rate gets too large, there are too many harmful mutations, and the species dies out.

A subtle but important point is that the *information* must be stable, not the DNA itself. That is, a mutation that doesn't alter the proteins produced by the DNA is irrelevant. (We saw a similar effect with the joke about St. Peter escorting new arrivals into Heaven: The central concept, the funny part, was unchanged even with very different versions of the joke.)

In addition, the DNA's information must be able to change (mutate). This is paradoxical because it conflicts with the need for stability, yet both are true. The mutation rate of DNA must be high enough that the species can adapt at least as quickly as its environment changes, yet low enough that the harmful changes don't doom the species. Species that didn't mutate quickly enough aren't around any more.

Finally, the DNA must contain the means for its own reproduction. If the individuals of the species don't reproduce, it's a quick end for the DNA.

Now consider the disadvantages that go along with evolution of the genes encoded in your DNA.

Evolution is *slow*. Each mutation inevitably starts in one individual, and then the gene for the newly evolved trait or altered feature must propagate through that individual's descendants to a large fraction of the population over dozens, hundreds, or thousands of generations, as it slowly replaces the less-adapted trait. A rapid event, such as a sudden ice age, a new competing species arriving from overseas, or a deadly disease, takes place much too fast for evolution to handle, and often results in extinction.

And worse, evolution is *random*. There's no guiding hand, no intent, no motivation. Mutations are far more likely to be bad than good. This amplifies the slowness of the evolutionary process: Not only does it take a long time for a mutation to take hold, but "good" mutations are few and far between, so most mutations just die out.

And finally, the filtering mechanism for mutations is very harsh: Death. That is, an individual with an unsuccessful mutation either dies right away, or loses the "survival of the fittest" competition in the long run. There's no way to say, "Oops, this mutation of my DNA was a bad idea, let's go back to the better version of this gene." Once a bad mutation occurs, that's it.

So "traditional evolution," the mutation of DNA and the harsh filtering by nature, is a slow process, one that works well over long time spans but can't respond to rapid changes, where "sudden" means "faster than a few dozen generations," and it is helpless in the face of catastrophes.

The Speedy Alternative

Some people are quick to criticize cliches, but what is a cliche? It is a truth that has retained its validity through time. Mankind would lose half its hard-earned wisdom, built up patiently over the ages, if it ever lost its cliches.
– Marvin G. Gregory

Where does human language – memetics – come into this picture? Evolution has a remarkable way of solving *very* hard problems: Consider the human eye, the rattlesnake's venom, the frigate bird's ability to soar for a week over the deep ocean without landing, and the penguin's ability to survive, breed and thrive in Antarctica. These, and countless other amazing results of natural selection, illustrate how the inexorable forces of evolution can "try, try again" until amazing solutions are found to the problem of survival.

One of the hard problems is evolution itself: It is slow and cumbersome. Imagine there are two nearly identical groups of primates, but one of these groups is somehow able to evolve faster, and with fewer harmful mutations. As the weather changes, new diseases arrive, competition increases, and so on, the fast-evolving group will have an advantage over the other group: They can develop warmer fur faster, develop immunity faster, or learn to match new competition faster than the other group. It wouldn't take long at all for the faster-evolving primates to supplant the ordinary primates.

Which is to say, the *ability to evolve quickly* is itself an evolutionary advantage, as long as it's not accompanied by harmful mutations. If evolution can speed up, while simultaneously avoiding harmful changes, it would be a *huge* advantage to a species.

That is exactly what happened, and what language and memes are all about. In a weird twist of logic, evolution created a better, faster version of itself, by using memes to pass information from one generation to the next, rather than genes. Evolution *reinvented itself*, in the form of information that is passed culturally rather than genetically, yet is still subject to the principles of Evolution Science! In other words:

Memes are evolution's way of improving itself.

We have emphasized several times that it's the *information* in your DNA that is important, not the DNA itself. The act of procreation is, at its core, the act of copying information. Memes are just a more effective way to do what DNA and RNA have been doing for a few billion years: replicate information.

Let's compare the evolution of memes and genes in more detail. Why are memes better?

Intentional Memes

For me the Jewish religion like all others is an incarnation of the most childish superstitions.
– Albert Einstein, January 3, 1954, in a letter to the philosopher Eric Gutkind

Unlike DNA, the evolution of memes is not necessarily random. It is common for people to deliberately and knowingly craft a meme for a particular purpose. Consider the song, *I'd Like to Teach the World to Sing*, a song advertising Coca Cola® (by songwriters Cook and Greenaway). Although most of us hate "ad jingles," this song became a hit in its own right, particularly in the United Kingdom where it is one of the best selling one hundred singles of all time. The Coca Cola company couldn't have asked for a cheaper way to get its message across: People paid money to listen to their ad! This may be one of the best advertising memes in history, and is often credited with helping the Coca Cola company, which had come under severe competitive pressure from Pepsi®, regain its position as the number one soft drink in America. *I'd Like to Teach the World to Sing* is a set of intertwined memes, one that makes it reproduce (it's a very nice, catchy song), and the other that carries a commercial message.

In the last decade, this type of marketing has even gotten a name, "viral marketing." The advertising industry is always at the forefront of sociology, always ready to exploit the latest insights into human behavior so that they can sell more stuff. The Madison-Avenue marketing experts were quick to grasp the power of memes and memetics, and turn it into a tool of the trade. "Viral Marketing" is the technique of creating an advertising campaign that carries within it something so appealing that people tell it to one another with no further expense or effort from the advertisers. A viral marketing campaign centers on a self-replicating idea, a meme, that carries the advertiser's message *and* carries the mechanism for its own reproduction. The Coca Cola song wasn't the first viral marketing campaign, but it was one of the best.

Viral marketing illustrates our point that meme mutations aren't always accidental or random. Unlike genes, memes can be deliberately created and improved.

Bad Memes Aren't Fatal

Pryor's Observation: How long you live has nothing to do with how long you are going to be dead.

In 1960, Professor Timothy Leary of Harvard University's Psychology Department, traveled to Cuernavaca, Mexico. There, he joined some native people in a religious ceremony that included the use of psilocybin mushrooms, a natural and very powerful hallucinogenic drug. The experience, according to Dr. Leary, taught him more in a few hours about the psychology of the human brain than he'd learned in the previous fifteen years.

At the time, psychedelics like psilocybin mushrooms and LSD were legal, and the use of these drugs by researchers and psychologists was considered quite legitimate. Leary was so impressed by these drugs and the insights it gave him, that it altered the course of his life, and of American history. He became a counterculture icon, a vocal, articulate and flamboyant advocate of mind-altering drugs, and a hero of the 1960s anti-establishment, anti-war movement. Ultimately, Leary became an international fugitive, was imprisoned several times, and was finally freed by California governor Jerry Brown.

Millions of people in the 1960s "hippie" generation around the world tried, or regularly used, the psychedelic drugs that Leary advocated. Although Leary wasn't single-handedly responsible for the "Psychedelic Drug meme" and the consequent popularity of LSD, he certainly was a strong influence.

LSD seemed like a good idea to many people in the 1960s, but in retrospect it's pretty obvious that long-term use of such drugs is harmful. Luckily for most LSD users, this meme wasn't fatal. Some users experience frightening "bad trips," but the effects are rarely permanent.

Unlike a DNA mutation, which is passed to one's offspring, a human mind can accept, and then later reject, a meme, as long as the human body survives the ordeal.

One of the dark secrets of those who came of age during the 1960s, one that they work hard to conceal from their adolescent children, is that many of them tried these drugs in their youth. In the 1960s, and well into the 1970s, it was a rare college party that didn't include the pungent aroma of marijuana, and the use of stronger drugs was common. But most of these same people later in life rejected the *Psychedelic Drug* meme for what it is: A bad idea. And they didn't have to *die* to get rid of this meme.

High-Bandwidth Evolution

> *But a short time elapsed after the death of the great reformer of the Jewish religion, before his principles were departed from by those who professed to be his special servants, and perverted into an engine for enslaving mankind, and aggrandizing their oppressors in Church and State.*
> *– Thomas Jefferson, in a letter to S. Kercheval, 1810*

The final advantage of meme evolution over genes is the sheer amount of information that can be passed. The human genome contains roughly 25,000 protein-encoding genes, which is a lot of information. But the amount of knowledge that can be passed genetically is tiny, just a fraction of the knowledge that one can learn in a lifetime via memes.

Consider the types of knowledge that are encoded genetically (that is, instinctive knowledge). Birds can migrate for thousands of miles. A salmon can roam the whole ocean, and then return to the exact same river, tributary, stream, and finally, the little creek, where it was hatched. A spider can weave a beautiful web. A penguin knows that when a storm is approaching, it must huddle with other penguins or freeze to death.

The list of amazing instincts goes on an on. But far more remarkable is the human ability to describe, with great accuracy, *all* of these behaviors, and to pass the knowledge to friends, students, neighbors, and children, with high fidelity, and to maintain this information for many generations, even for millennia.

Consider skills like writing, engineering, poetry, warfare, farming, or music. It is almost inconceivable that these traits could evolve without language. Memes can carry far more information than genes.

Meme Stability

Children are naive – they trust everyone. School is bad enough, but, if you put a child anywhere in the vicinity of a church, you're asking for trouble.
– Frank Zappa

Recall that stability is one of the most important traits of your DNA – the information must be passed reliably. Because of this, our bodies have some remarkable biochemistry that protects our DNA from damage, and certain kinds of damage can even be repaired. Is the same thing true of memes?

The human mind seems to be uniquely programmed for exactly this purpose: meme stability. During childhood, we are able to absorb vast amounts of information about the world, our friends and neighbors, and how to survive and make a living. Robert Fulgham's fun and insightful book, *All I Really Need to Know I Learned in*

Kindergarten is remarkably true – all of the really important stuff is taught to us at a very young age, and we never forget it.

Children seem to go through a wide-open phase where they can be taught just about anything (even some wildly implausible stuff), and they'll accept it. One of the joys of parenthood is watching a child explore the world, trying everything. Toddlers will watch, feel, smell, pick up, and even eat, just about everything they find. A five year old is so full of questions it can drive a parent crazy. Children love to emulate their parents; they can spend hours or days in "mimic play," playing house, hunting, fishing, fighting, and even with young romances.

But when the child grows into an adult, beliefs become entrenched. The wide open library of a child's mind, which yearns to absorb new volumes, seems to turn into a dusty, locked archive. Some new information can go in, especially if it agrees with the information that's already there, but most of a person's fundamental beliefs become almost unassailable by age eighteen. It is *very* difficult to alter an adult's opinions. Fulgham's *Kindergarten* title quoted above, and St. Ignatius' famous quote, "Give me the boy, and I'll give you the man," are both reflections of this fact: If you want to teach fundamental beliefs, you have to teach the children, because by the time a person is an adult, it's usually too late.

This makes evolutionary sense. If biological evolution has "reinvented itself" in the form of memes, as a better way to pass information from one generation to the next, then we would expect the human mind to be programmed for reliability. And that's exactly what we see: As the child matures and becomes an adult, the mind "solidifies," resistant to new ideas, and protects the fidelity of the ideas it absorbed during youth.

Memes thus pass the test of *reliability*, in that like DNA, information can be passed down through many generations accurately. This is critical to human survival. Locations of food, good ways to hunt, the procedures for making tools, clothing, and weapons, all must be passed from one generation to the next if the species is to survive. During most of human history, the average lifespan was much shorter than it is today, probably in the neighborhood of twenty-five to forty years. That means that by the time a human reached the age of twenty, his or her parents might be dead. If you didn't remember the lessons you'd learned from them, so that you could pass them to your children, those lessons would be lost forever.

So it's no surprise that our brains are "hard wired" to have a period of open acceptance of ideas (our childhood, when the memes are "loaded" into our brains), followed by an entrenchment of ideas (our adulthood) where we're reluctant to alter our beliefs, and work hard to pass our knowledge to our children accurately.

Memes: One of Evolution's "Good Tricks"

I personally think we developed language because of our deep need to complain.
– Lily Tomlin

The human ability to speak is nothing more than evolution's way of improving on itself: It's a better way to pass information. It is faster, far more adaptable and flexible than genetic mutation, and can pass far more intricate information from one generation to the next than is possible with genes. An ice age? No problem, humans learn to use other animals' hides for warmth. A competing species? No problem, a few humans can find a way to defeat the competitor, and in *one generation*, pass that information to all humans. Disease? Instead of relying on immune systems, humans *invent drugs* to improve their survival.

Cultural evolution has all of the advantages of Darwin's process of Natural Selection: Complex solutions can arise without any conscious design. At the same time, memes don't suffer from the glacial trial-and-error process that makes genetic evolution so slow and cumbersome.

Memes have proved to be the most important adaptive trait in the history of life on Earth. No other animal comes even close to humans in terms of adaptability and rapid progress. Humans live virtually everywhere on Earth, including a few who live undersea and in orbit above the atmosphere. Humans lifespan is vastly increased. Over half of all children used to die, now the mortality rate is just a small percent. The human population has swelled from a few millions to over six billion (6×10^9) in just a few centuries, and our impact on the environment is so severe that one of the largest mass extinctions in the Earth's entire four billion year history is currently underway.

This extreme adaptability is a direct result of evolution's "trick" of reinventing itself in the form of memes, bits of cultural information that follow Darwin's evolutionary principles, but in a new, better way.

We talk because memes are better than genes for evolution.

Interlude: A Prayer

O Lord our God, help us to tear their soldiers to bloody shreds with our shells;

help us to cover their smiling fields with the pale forms of their patriot dead;

help us to drown the thunder of the guns with the wounded, writhing in pain;

help us to lay waste their humble homes with a hurricane of fire;

help us to wring the hearts of their unoffending widows with unavailing grief;

help us to turn them out roofless with their little children to wander unfriended through wastes of their desolated land in rags and hunger and thirst, sport of the sun-flames of summer and the icy winds of winter, broken in spirit, worn with travail, imploring Thee for the refuge of the grave and denied it --

for our sakes, who adore Thee, Lord, blast their hopes, blight their lives, protract their bitter pilgrimage, make heavy their steps, water their way with their tears, stain the white snow with the blood of their wounded feet!

We ask of one who is the Spirit of love and who is the ever-faithful refuge and friend of all that are sore beset, and seek His aid with humble and contrite hearts.

Grant our prayer, O Lord, and Thine shall be the praise and honor and glory now and ever, Amen.

Mark Twain (1835-1910) - War Prayer

6. Religion's Immunity System

It seems that anything worth having is also worth stealing, and therefore worth defending: A tree has thick bark to keep out bugs; your body has a complex immune system to battle disease; a landowner erects a fence to protect his property; a country posts soldiers on its borders to keep out invaders. These are all examples of the same thing: Immunity systems that have evolved (either biologically or culturally) to protect the things of value that help us survive and prosper.

The memes we've studied thus far have focused on the core beliefs of Jews, Muslims and Christians, ideas like monotheism, sin and guilt, heaven and hell, and the origin of morals. These are the "core theology" memes that assert Yahweh's existence, powers, and laws.

While these core-theology memes were evolving, a second set of memes was developing in parallel: Religion's "immune system," the memes that defend and support the core theology. In this chapter, we will go back to pre-Christian times again, and work our way forward, learning about these "militant" memes and how they enhanced the growth and spread of western religions.

The Anti-Rationalism Meme

Question with boldness even the existence of God; because, if there is one, he must more approve of the homage of reason than that of blindfolded faith.
–Thomas Jefferson

From the philosopher's chair, all religions have a problem: They can't be proved true or false. That is, the foundation of every religion ultimately must be accepted on faith.

This faith-based foundation can be illustrated as follows:

Q: "How do you know God exists?"

A: "Because the Bible tells me so."

Q: "Who wrote the Bible?"

A: "A bunch of people, but they were writing God's literal words."

Q: "And how do you know these people didn't make mistakes?"

A: "Because God wrote the Bible."

Q: "So God wrote the book that proves His existence?"

... and so on, around and around in a circle of logic that ultimately can only end with faith.

Roughly 2,500 years ago, the Greek Rationalists had already considered, and firmly rejected, this sort of circular reasoning. The Greeks realized that to prove something true, you had to base your proof on some deeper truth, to start with known facts, and use them to illuminate the unknown. It simply wouldn't do to take two unproved facts, and use each to "prove" the other (such as God writing the Bible, and the Bible proving God's existence).

When the Greeks began to colonize the lands of the Jews in the fourth century BCE, the two cultures mixed, and the Jews began to study Greek Rationalism. By this time, the Jews were firmly convinced that their laws came from Yahweh through Moses. The Greeks, on the other hand, had a well-developed philosophy that derived moral guidelines from natural principles. When the Greeks encountered Jewish culture and law, they were fascinated by it, especially by the Jews' tradition of a written religion and written laws. But the Greeks rejected the Jewish view that ethics came only from Yahweh. Judaism was incompatible with their polytheistic beliefs, Judaism's claim that ethics came from God wasn't compatible with the behavior of the Greeks' own gods (who were not particularly well behaved!), and Jewish ethics weren't compatible with their Rational philosophy.

There was a very subtle, but critical, logical problem with the Jews' god-given morals, a circularity that Plato discovered. Plato argued: If something is good or bad because Yahweh approves, then how can Yahweh know what to approve? Yahweh himself has no rules to go by – something is good or bad *because* Yahweh approves of it. In other words, good or bad originates with Yahweh, and there is no foundation. Yahweh could decide that infanticide was good, and that would *make* it good, and because it was good, Yahweh would approve of it. According to Plato, Yahweh himself was caught in a circular argument. This was contrary to the Greek Rationalists position, who believed that all ethics had to have a foundation.

The Greeks had developed the idea that certain laws of logic were so strong that even gods couldn't violate them. For example, we know that one plus one is two, and even a god can't make it otherwise. Likewise, even a god has to have a foundation on which to decide whether something is ethical or not – he can't just decide, or else he falls into Plato's trap of circular ethics. Good and bad, according to Rationalists, must come from the human condition and human happiness.

As time went by, the Jewish philosophers and rabbis absorbed Hellenic culture and philosophy, and the rationalist logic began to creep into Jewish discourse. To some, the very foundations of the Jewish faith appeared to be shaky. The Jews had a big problem on their hands. Everything about Yahweh, from his authority to his very existence, was in question.

The solution was a new meme, one that undermined the credibility of Greek Rational Philosophy. Within a century or so of the Greek invasion, the *Anti Rationalism* meme had arisen. This meme asserts that logical thinking is a misguided approach to truth, that you have to have *faith*, and feel the truth with your *heart*, not in your head. The *Anti-Rationalism* meme asserts that logic and rational thought are not the path to truth, and that they in fact lead you away from the truth.

"Divine revelation, not reason, is the source of all truth."
– Tertullian of Carthage (150-225 AD)

In other words, the mysteries of Yahweh were beyond human understanding and logic, only acts of faith could bring understanding. The *Anti Rationalism* meme essentially solved the Jew's problem, and skirted Plato's logic trap. Rather than trying to prove the existence of Yahweh by logic, you must feel him in your heart. Rather than proving that the ethics of the Ten Commandments have a natural, logical foundation based on human happiness, you pray to Yahweh for guidance and truth. The problems of Greek philosophy were swept aside, and difficulties revealed by Greek Rationalism could be dismissed. The Jews, and later the Christians and Muslims, were safe again.

The Hellenic invasion of the Middle East sparked the *Anti Rationalism* meme, but its evolution didn't stop there. Two thousand years gave it plenty of time to mature and spread. Consider these more modern versions of the meme.

> *Although the Divinely infused light of faith is more powerful than the natural light of reason, nevertheless in our present state we only imperfectly participate in it...*
> *– St. Thomas Aquinas (1225-1274)*

St. Thomas' version of the *Anti Rationalism* meme is improved in the sense that even our faith is suspect; we can have faith, but it is imperfect. Then consider the Roman Catholic Church's more modern statement:

> *The Catholic Church has always held that there is a twofold order of knowledge, and that these two orders are distinguished from one another not only in their principle but in their object; in one we know by natural reason, in the other by Divine faith; the object of the one is truth attainable by natural reason, the object of the other is mysteries hidden in God, but which we have to believe and which can only be known to us by Divine revelation.*
> *-- Catholic Encyclopedia*

The Roman Catholic version of the meme clearly separates knowledge into two categories: That which can be understood by reason, and that which must be accepted on faith.

Even more fascinating is this statement:

*[It] is possible that God has reasons for allowing evil to
exist that we simply cannot understand. In this the Christian
can have confidence in God knowing that His ways are
above our ways (Isaiah 55:8-9).*
-- *Christian Apologetics & Research Ministry, www.car-
m.org*

The one, from the Christian Apologetics, makes a bold assertion
that even our logic is flawed! There may be logic that is higher than
human logic, so no matter how smart we are, Yahweh may be
smarter, and no amount of human reasoning can disprove anything
about religion that might appear to be irrational. That is a *very* powerful variant on the *Anti Rationalism* meme; it not only says that
faith triumphs logic, but in addition, our logical abilities are suspect
and can't be trusted.

The Ignorance-Is-Bliss Meme

*To surrender to ignorance and call it God has always been
premature, and it remains premature today.*
– *Isaac Asimov*

In 2008, the California Court of Appeals issued a surprising
ruling that home schooling of children was illegal unless the teacher
(usually the parents) were qualified, licensed schoolteachers. This
caused an absolute firestorm of protest, from parents, the State
Superintendent of Public Schools, and even the governor himself.
But the loudest protests came from Christian organizations, who
made statements equating the decision to an attack on Christianity
itself.

The same Appeals Court overturned its own decision a few
weeks later, but the firestorm caused by this short-lived decision
turned a spotlight on the true motivations of many home-school families: They are avoiding secular teaching to prevent their children
from leaving the Christian, Jewish or Muslim religions. A widespread rumor, repeated often by Christian writers, claims that *eighty-
five percent of public-schooled children leave the faith.*

Conservative Christians, Jews and Muslims share a deep-seated fear of modern physics, chemistry, biology, geology, anthropology and history, because their millennia-old religions don't square with modern knowledge. Most of the sacred texts of the Abrahamic religions were "frozen" into their approximate current forms somewhere between 2,800 years ago (the Jewish Tanakh) and 1,400 years ago (the Qur'an), yet civilization and science have made huge advances in virtually all branches of knowledge. Naturally there are statements in these sacred texts that don't agree with modern discoveries, and experience has shown that exposure to these modern ideas is dangerous. It leads people, especially young adults, away from religion.

To protect their children and keep them "in the fold," they teach their children at home, thereby controlling their children's access to knowledge that conflicts with their beliefs.

This is an example of the *Ignorance Is Bliss* meme in action. This meme evolved to defend religion against knowledge that conflicts with religious teachings. In a nutshell, it declares, "Everything I need to know is in the Bible." It comes in various strengths; a few people make the strong claim that the the Tanakh, Bible or Qur'an contains all important knowledge, but most allow the teaching of subjects that don't conflict with the sacred texts.

In 1966, the Roman Catholic Church formally ended the largest censorship drive in the history of the world, formally known as the *Index Librorum Prohibitorum* (the *Index of Forbidden Books*). Formally launched in 1559 under Pope Paul IV, this four-century project was remarkably successful, even against non-Catholics. The Church was so powerful in Europe and America that many authors would avoid controversial topics, or modify their works according to the Church's dictates, in order to avoid condemnation by the Church. Authors who ignored the Church's dictates and were banned had trouble finding publishers, and even if they were published, their books were often hard or impossible to find because bookstores were under pressure not to stock them.

The *Ignorance Is Bliss* meme goes back much farther than 1559, though. Book burnings, the rejection of the non-canonical Gospels (the gospels of Jesus that were not accepted as part of the New Testament at the Council of Nicaea), suppression of scientific findings such as the discoveries of Copernicus and Galileo – these are all further examples of the *Ignorance Is Bliss* meme. Censorship, and its close cousin, disinformation (such as government-sponsored propaganda), are probably as old as writing itself, and perhaps older. Virtually every organization and institution practices it to a certain degree, ranging from a "spin doctor" for a political candidate, movie star or corporation, to government military secrets, to the overt censorship practiced by repressive governments such as China and North Korea. But nothing comes close to the censorship imposed by religions throughout history.

Even though the Roman Catholic *Index Librorum Prohibitorum* is officially ended, censorship of anti-religious writings is hardly a thing of the past. As I write these words, a centuries-long war in America's schools to halt teaching of Evolution Science rages on. The most famous battle in this war was the 1925 "Scopes Monkey Trial," fought in a courtroom in rural Tennessee, which was a legal defeat for evolution (the judge ruled that banning evolution in science courses didn't favor any religion), but a public-relations victory for science. It wasn't until 1968 that the United States Supreme Court finally ruled that a ban on teaching evolution *was* in fact unconstitutional because its primary purpose was religious. For a while, it looked like science had won the day; creationism was banned outright from all public-school curricula, and evolution science was taught in most science classes. But Creationists invented a new, pseudo-scientific spin called "intelligent design," which again threatens the foundation of science education in America. By teaching Creationism in the guise of science, America's Christian conservatives are again attempting to censor Darwin's Theory of Evolution, not by directly prohibiting it, but by dilution and confusion.

The Inerrancy Meme

> *The Bible is the inerrant ... word of the living God. It is*
> *absolutely infallible, without error in all matters pertaining*
> *to faith and practice, as well as in areas such as geography,*
> *science, history, etc.*
> -- *The Reverend Jerry Falwell*

The gods of ancient religions were remarkably fluid and change-able. Not the gods themselves, but rather the *concepts* (the meme-plexes that describe each god); stories would travel from region to region, from person to person, changing and combining, and thereby changing the very nature of the gods themselves. This *syncretic* process, the melding and blending of beliefs and mythological sto-ries as cultures met and mixed, is at the heart of how memes and cul-tural evolution work.

The gods Zeus and Jupiter are a perfect example of this. Ini-tially, both were sky gods, and wielded thunderbolts when angry, but they had little else in common. Zeus, like all early Greek gods, was a personal, flesh-and-blood god with many human flaws, but super-natural powers. The Roman god Jupiter started of as an animistic spirit, more of a symbol of the heavenly light, without a flesh-and-blood body and no human-like personality at all. Jupiter was ... boring. There were no lurid stories, no tales to amaze wide-eyed Roman children, no moral lessons to be learned from the bland Jupiter.

The Romans first learned about Greek gods through their Etr-uscan neighbors, and via Greek colonization of southern Italy around the eighth century BCE. The Greeks' Olympian gods were much more interesting than their Roman counterparts, and as we've learned from our studies of memetic evolution, became the "winners," the survivors. But it was more of a merging of gods than an outright replacement: Most of the Greek gods had existing counterparts in the Roman religion, and Jupiter more or less assumed Zeus' identity, taking on all of the great mythological stories that the Greeks had been telling for centuries. By the end of the assimilation, most of the

Zeus-mythology memes had attached themselves to Jupiter, making the two gods indistinguishable. Jupiter managed to keep his name, but little else.

The Greeks and Romans were not unusual in this regard; the Israelites' early theology was subject to this same evolutionary, syncretic process. For example, the story of Noah's flood was recorded by the scribes of Mari (part of modern Syria) on stone tablets that date to almost 2,000 years BCE, except that in Mari legend it is King Gilgamesh, not Noah, who built the ark. Both Genesis and Gilgamesh stories include building an ark, a disastrous flood, riding out the flood in the ark, sending birds to discover dry land, and an offering of thanks when everyone was safe on dry land.

This evolutionary process came to a screeching halt when the Jews invented the idea of a *written* religion. Jewish tradition say that the Torah was dictated to Moses by God himself, but history shows that starting around 850-800 BCE, two writers known as the "Jehovist" and the "Elohist" began collecting the Jewish stories and writing them down. The Elohist, a Levite priest, wrote major parts of Genesis, Exodus and Numbers. The Jehovist was probably a woman, and *not* a priest, yet was the most prolific of the biblical authors. Her works include a great deal of Genesis, Joshua, Judges, 1Samuel, 2Samuel and Kings, and she probably contributed to Exodus, Numbers and Deuteronomy.

The Jehovist and Elohist were followed by the "Priestly source" (around 700 BCE), the "Deuteronomist" (around 600 BCE) and the "Redactor" (around 400-375 BCE). Most scholars agree that these five, often abbreviated as E, J, P, D and R, were the authors of most of the written stories that became the Torah, but there is dissension; some argue that the Torah is a compilation of many smaller texts. Either way, most scholars agree that these text were written some time in the period from around 900-300 BCE.

The real birth of *The Inerrancy* meme was the Great Assembly of Jewish scholars and scribes around 450 BCE. According to Jewish tradition, the Men of the Great Assembly compiled the contents of the Tanakh into its current form, which has remained largely unchanged ever since. Modern scholars say that the contents of the Tanakh continued to evolve for several more centuries, reaching its nearly-final version around 200 BCE, and continuing with smaller changes for about four hundred more years.

This was one of the most significant events in the history of religion. For the first time, there was a canonical scripture, a list of the "correct" word of God. All of the writings that were not included in the Tanakh were called *false* – they had been examined and rejected by the Men of the Great Assembly. Moreover, the Torah, which is the most sacred and central part of the Tanakh, was said to be *written by Moses himself* under God's direct inspiration. In other words, the Torah was God's own words, perfect and without errors of any kind. It was the birth of the *Inerrancy* meme.

The birth of Christianity was a remarkable echo of this same history. After Jesus' death sometime around 30 CE, his life and deeds became oral legends that circulated among the nascent Christian community. Like the Jewish stories of the Torah, the stories of Jesus' life were subject to the syncretic forces of human culture: Folklore and stories from far before Jesus' time were stirred into the pot, turning the man from a teacher and nonconformist into a demigod and later into Yahweh incarnate.

However, the oral period was short; the Jews' well-established tradition of a written religion meant that the early Christians (who were still Jewish) started putting the stories to paper. This continued for a couple centuries, until the Council of Nicaea, just like its predecessor at the Great Assembly, selected a few writings from the many dozens about Jesus' life, and declared these, and only these, to be the canonical scriptures, the correct scriptures, the *inerrant* word of God himself. The works of the Council's dissenters were confiscated and burned, so as not to corrupt and confuse "true" Christians.

The *Inerrancy* meme remained fairly static, doing its work but not changing much, until the late nineteenth century. The middle ages and the Renaissance brought the rediscovery of the the Greek Rationalists, and huge leaps forward in logic and mathematics. Intellectual giants like philosophers René Descartes and Shahab al-

Din Suhrawardi were so excited by the successes of the modern logic that they tried to apply it to religion, "proving" that God exists through a series of deductive and inductive steps, based on known facts.

In the early nineteenth century, a second generation of modern philosophers began applying these same logic principles to "prove" the inerrancy of the Bible. This movement peaked in 1976, when Harold Lindsell's *The Battle for the Bible* was published, a book that was heavily critical of anyone who doubted the Bible's inerrancy. Lindsell asserted that belief in inerrancy was the true measure of an evangelical Christian, that those not willing to assert the Bible's inerrancy were not true believers. Most mainstream Christians considered Lindsell's ideas divisive, and he made the matter worse by attacking, by name, many individual Christian leaders and entire churches.

Regardless of Lindsell's motivations or methods, the topic of inerrancy is still one of the most important issues in Christianity, as well as Judaism and Islam. Dozens of papers are written every year, and thousands of web sites discuss the all aspects of the topic.

The *Inerrancy* meme continues to do its work. Its most important target by far is the Evolution Science itself, which is one of the few sciences that directly and obviously conflicts with biblical teaching. But it also enters into discussions of morality and laws, such as whether homosexual marriage should be allowed; opponents of gay marriage point to Genesis (Sodom and Gomorrah) and Leviticus, and since the Bible is inerrant, there can be no further discussion.

Successful memes are often "stolen" and incorporated into other religions, and the *Inerrancy* meme is no exception. When the Prophet Mohammad recited the words of the Qur'an to his scribe, he was said to be acting as Allah's own voice, speaking Allah's very words. Since Allah is perfect in every way, and the Qur'an is Allah's own words, there can be no mistakes in the Qur'an according to Islamic beliefs.

The *Inerrancy* meme adds considerable weight to the authority of the Tanakh, the Bible, and the Qur'an. Without it, any particular passage of scripture is open to interpretation, and the faithful have the option of questioning the authenticity of anything they like. Nothing can be certain. But when the *Inerrancy* meme is added, the scriptures become final in every way. If something is written, it is God's own words, and that is the end of it.

The Martyrdom Meme

Martyrdom is the only way in which a man can become famous without ability.
– George Bernard Shaw (1856-1950)

Suicide bombing is one of the greatest plagues of the modern world. Every day, it seems we read of another fanatical "martyr" who blows himself up (it's almost always men), along with dozens or hundreds of innocent bystanders who are killed or injured. These men believe that their martyrdom will get them the Golden Ticket to Heaven, and what a Heaven! Fountains, all you can eat, and seventy-two virgins. Not only seventy-two virgins, but the man himself will never run out of sexual energy taking care of all these virgins, and best of all, after each encounter, the young lady who enjoyed the martyr's attentions becomes a virgin again! Or so we are told.

Ironically, these men are not martyrs at all, at least not by almost any mainstream religion's definition. The term "martyr" means one who is killed or suffers greatly for religious beliefs or principles, usually for refusing to renounce his or her beliefs, or refusing to pay homage to another deity. Unlike the suicide bombers, true martyrs simply are true to their faith, even at the cost of their lives. True martyrs don't seek death, and they certainly don't kill innocents as part of their martyrdom.

The *Martyrdom* meme is another of the powerful survival mechanisms that have evolved as part of the Religion Virus. Religions are in a constant competition with one another, and part of that competition has for time immemorial involved coercion and persecution.

Centuries before the time of Jesus, the Jews suffered at the hands of the Greeks when they refused to break Jewish laws, including execution for observing the Sabbath, or for refusing to honor the pagan gods of the Greek government. In a sense, martyrdom was a side effect of the Jew's *Monotheism* meme, because prior to the idea of monotheism, people had no problem paying homage to other gods – it was simply a sign of respect, and the various gods weren't particularly jealous of one another. But as we saw earlier in our studies, monotheism practically invites persecution in a polytheistic society.

Thus, martyrdom was an inevitable side effect of monotheism. By refusing to participate in the paganism of the time, the Jews practically invited trouble to their doorsteps, and persecution became a serious threat to the Yahweh memeplex. Religions have adapted various mechanism to resist coercion, some of which we studied with the *Heaven/Hell* memes (great rewards/punishment for making the right/wrong choice), and the *Guilt* meme. The *Martyrdom* meme added another weapon in the Religion Virus' arsenal to resist coercion: Those who die as Martyrs are exalted.

The Jews had a solid *Martyrdom* meme before Jesus arrived on the scene, but Jesus refined and exalted the concept in his Sermon on the Mount:

> *Blessed are those who are persecuted because of righteousness, for theirs is the kingdom of heaven. Blessed are you when people insult you, persecute you and falsely say all kinds of evil against you because of me. Rejoice and be glad, because great is your reward in heaven...*
> *– Matthew 5:10-12*

> *You have heard that it was said, 'Love your neighbor and hate your enemy.' But I tell you: Love your enemies and pray for those who persecute you, that you may be sons of your Father in heaven.*
> *– Matthew 5:43-45*

This is a marvelous meme. It tells Christians that the worse things get, the better off they are! This was especially important

during the earliest days of Christianity when it was a minority out-
lawed religion, and persecutions were common. Christians who
were suffering greatly for their faith needed every bit of help they
could get. The *Heaven* meme was a good start, but the *Martyrdom*
meme really gave Christians something to hold on to when all
seemed lost.

And it must have worked, because the Christians became noto-
rious for their stubbornness. Tertullian (~155-230 AD), a Christian
leader and prolific writer, describes a group of Christians in Ephesus
(an ancient city of what is now the Izmir Province of Turkey) who
begged for martyrdom from the Romans. The Roman officials executed a few but, according to Tertullian, the rest were sent away with
the admonition, "Miserable creatures, if you really wish to die, you
have precipices and halters enough."

Consider the Roman Catholic Church's official version of the
Martyrdom meme:

> ... *those who suffer death for the sake of the faith without
> having received Baptism are baptized by their death for and
> with Christ. This Baptism of blood, like the desire for Bap-
> tism, brings about the fruits of Baptism without being a
> sacrament.*
> – *Catholic Church, Catechism of the Catholic Church, Part
> Two, Chapter 1, Article 1, "The Sacrament of Baptism"*

The *Martyrdom* meme has served religion very well indeed over
the years. It comes in many forms; each of the three major Abrahamic religion has various definitions for *martyr*, but the underlying
idea – that those who suffer or die for their faith are rewarded in
Heaven – is universal. The *Martyrdom* meme helped Judaism,
Christianity, and Islam all survive, and even thrive, during times of
terrible persecution.

The various forms of the *Martyrdom* meme also illustrate one of
the most interesting benefits of using a *meme theory* point of view to
study religion. We started this section talking about suicide
bombers, and how most Americans believe that Islamic suicide
bombers are from impoverished, uneducated backgrounds and are

seduced into blowing themselves up by the "72 virgins in paradise" promise. In fact, many scholars have noted that this profile is wrong; that many suicide bombers are motivated by political, not religious, beliefs, and many are well-educated and from the middle class or even wealthy. But the American stereotype *suicide bomber meme* is itself an example of the "survival of the fittest" principle: For some reason, Americans like to believe this. They don't want to know that the hatred of American foreign policy is much more complex, and has its roots far back in the history of European imperialism. Americans would rather believe that anyone who hates them is somehow deranged, that their hatred can't possibly be rational. The "72 virgins" meme is much more likable to Americans, because it lets us off the hook. The "72 virgins" meme's survival *doesn't depend on whether it's true or not*, only that it has appeal to Americans.

The Underdog Meme

I never saw, heard, nor read, that the clergy were beloved in any nation where Christianity was the religion of the country. Nothing can render them popular, but some degree of persecution.
– Jonathan Swift

The *Underdog* meme takes advantage of the fact that persecuted people tend the stick together and defend one another. It is a close relative of the *Martyrdom* meme.

In George Orwell's groundbreaking novel *1984*, a totalitarian state keeps its proletariat masses in constant state of fear using surveillance, propaganda, and a constant state of war. The proletariat are taught to fear annihilation or worse at the hands of their enemies, and are kept off balance by the the constant threat of defeat. They work furiously to increase productivity for the war effort, and they don't question the oppressive policies of the government. In a war, you can't have dissent!

Orwell brilliantly captured one of humans' most primitive instincts: We draw together and act as a unit when threatened. This instinct goes back millions of years in history, long before humans even existed. Many social mammals, such as dogs, buffalo, and primates, will spend all sorts of time fighting with each other when all is well, but when an external threat, such as a predator, is detected, the animals will forget their differences and band together for the common defense of the group.

The Jews learned the value of persecution early in their history. The story of Exodus, which tells how the Israelites were driven from Egypt and forced to wander through the desert for generations, became an icon for the Jewish community's cohesiveness. Never mind that the story is probably a complete myth (unlike many other stories in the Torah, there is no archaeological evidence at all for Exodus). The story the Israelites' courage in the face of persecution and suffering are one of the most powerful and persistent memes of the Jewish and Christian religions.

The Christians were next. Their persecution at the hands of the Romans is legendary, never mind that they also persecuted each other viciously, a story that we told earlier. The persecution, cruel though it was, gave the Christians a rallying point, and brought them together into a cohesive, supportive group that few other events could have equaled.

The *Underdog* meme is religion's way of ensuring that, no matter how well things are actually going, people have to *think* they are being persecuted for their beliefs. In America today, a quick internet search for "Christian AND persecution" would make you think we'd returned to Roman times when Christians were being fed to the lions and torn apart by dogs. In spite of being by far the dominant religion in America, and enjoying more religious freedom than ever before in history, Christian writers constantly appear to be victims of persecution, discrimination, and ridicule.

This is another example of memetic evolution in action. The religions that adopted the *Underdog* meme, the habit of interpreting everything not in line with their dogma as an attack, have fared very well indeed. It keeps the "proletariat" off balance, and keeps the religious leaders in power. People are far more willing to follow a strong leader when they feel threatened; leaders are most vulnerable to challenges when they either fail completely, or when they bring prosperity and peace. Thus, even in times of peace and prosperity, Christians and Jews, and more recently Muslims, will maintain that they are under a constant attack, that their beliefs and way of life are threatened with extinction. They are the underdogs.

The One-Nation-Under-God Meme

Believing with you that religion is a matter which lies solely between Man and his G-d, I contemplate with sovereign reverence that act of the whole American people which declared that their legislature should 'make no law respecting an establishment of religion, or prohibiting the free exercise thereof,' thus building a wall of separation between church and state.
– Thomas Jefferson (1743-1826)

One of the most important meme-battles being waged today is for religious control of the American government. The so-called "religious right" is putting forth the idea that America was founded by Christians, for Christians, and that America should be a Christian country. On the surface, this seems like a plausible claim. According to the American Central Intelligence Agency (CIA), America religion breaks down like this for the year 2002:

78% Christian:
    52% Protestant
    24% Roman Catholic
    2% Mormon
12% Non-Christian:
    1% Jewish
    1% Muslim
    10% other
10% "none"

The Christians point to these numbers, and to the various mentions of the word "God" in our founding documents, and use these to bolster their claim that America was founded as a Christian nation, and that the secularism in today's government is a modern corruption of the founding principles of our great nation.

The government of the United States is not, in any sense, founded on the Christian religion.
– Article 11 of the Treaty of Tripoli, ratified by the United States Senate (June 7, 1797) and signed by President John Adams (June 10, 1797).

The Treaty of Tripoli, which was written during George Washington's presidency, ratified by the U.S. Senate, and signed by President John Adams, makes it clear that the founding fathers did *not* want a religious nation. This is in stark contrast with the religious right's revisionist history:

The idea that religion and politics don't mix was invented by the Devil to keep Christians from running their own country
– The Reverend Jerry Falwell

The most interesting aspect of this debate is that America's religious right has *convinced* many Americans that their version of history is true. This, in spite of the fact that America's "founding fathers" knew all too well the evils of faith-based government, having seen first hand the troubles it causes. They very carefully crafted America's constitution to keep America's government entirely secular. They were *not* anti-religious; quite the contrary. The purpose of keeping government secular was to *ensure* American's right to religious freedom. And it worked: Due to the foresight of those who wrote the constitution, almost all Americans can worship as they please. America has members of almost every religion in the world living and worshipping freely within its borders.

So one has to ask: *Why is the religious right so anxious to make ours a Christian, rather than secular, government?* After all, the secular Constitution guarantees Americans the right to worship – what more could they want? What is the problem? Why is this fundamental change to the government so important to these people?

The answer is simple: During the evolution of the modern religion memeplexes, one of the most successful memes is that religion should be an integral part of government. This is one of the "good tricks" of the evolution of the religion virus. Religions that have partnered with governments, or that *are* the government, are far more successful than religions that keep apart from government. In other words, this meme is a survivor, one of the memes that has made Christianity far more pervasive than it would have been otherwise. (This is true of all religions, particularly modern-day Islam, but for this section, we are focusing on Christianity in America.)

Religion and government have been intertwined for at least as long as written history. However, one particular influential writer, Aurelius Augustinus, known as Saint Augustine, put the justification down on paper as well as anyone in history. Since his writings are among the most influential in the history of the Christian churches, behind only Saint Paul, they're worth our attention. Augustine said that although the cities of men were of no consequence compared with the City of God, even so:

> *The church could not neglect the State, but must guide it to protect human beings from their own sinful natures. The state must employ repression and punishment to restrain people, who were inherently sinful, from destroying each other and the few good men and women that God had elected to save from hell.*
> – St. Augustine, City of God

The partnership of religion and government is a two-way street. Religion gets an enormous advantage if it is the law of the land – after all, you won't go to prison for murder or torture in the name of your religion if you are enforcing the law. And the government gains an enormous advantage by having God on its side. Whatever decisions the government makes can be God's own words; it's hard to argue that the government is wrong when its authority comes from God himself.

Thus, it is not surprising that America's Christian Right is anxious to have their version of Christianity and Christian morals embedded into the law of the land. Their religion has evolved this as one of its best memes.

The Synergy of the Immunity Memes

> *Clearly the person who accepts the Church as an infallible guide will believe whatever the Church teaches.*
> – Saint Thomas Aquinas

As with other groups of memes we've studied, the true power of the *Immunity* memes becomes apparent when we see them as a synergistic memeplex.

The *Anti-Rationalism* and *Ignorance-is-Bliss* memes work together to thwart rational thought and knowledge. Combined with the *Inerrancy* meme, which states that the scriptures are absolutely true, the faithful are taught to trust the Bible, trust their faith, and avoid logical thought and secular knowledge. These three memes form a memeplex that is much more powerful than any one of them individually.

The *Martyrdom* and *Underdog* memes work together to ensure that the faithful always feel persecuted, and yet that same persecution will be the key to infinite rewards in heaven.

The *One Nation Under God* meme works to ensure that religious beliefs become the law of the land, and that religious leaders become more powerful. It also works in conjunction with the *Anti-Rationalism* and *Inerrancy* memes to keep secular teaching away from the faithful, by ensuring that political laws are in agreement with religious beliefs.

The human body has developed a magnificent and diverse set of defenses to guard against all of the bacteria, viruses, parasites and other unpleasant creatures that would take advantage of us if they could. In a very parallel fashion, religions have evolved their own immune system, the *Immunity* memes, that attack foreign threats that might weaken the beliefs of the faithful.

Interlude: This Book

[In] this and all other well-governed Christian realmes, the cryme of blasphemy against God ... is a cryme of the highest nature, and ought to be severely punished ... with death.
– Proceedings against Thomas Aikenhead, Records of Justiciary in Edinburgh, A.D. 1696

I did not set out to write a book about religion. The seeds of this this book were planted twenty years ago while studying for my Master's Degree in Computer Science at Stanford University. I had the good fortune to take two classes in the computational aspects of natural language (syntax and semantics) from the brilliant Professor Winograd. At the same time I encountered Richard Dawkins' *Selfish Genes and Selfish Memes,* and Douglas Hofstadter's article, *On Viral Sentences and Self-Replicating Structures*, which introduced me to the fascinating concept of memes.

Professor Winograd made a very strong case that true artificial intelligence (AI – computers that can really think) will be beyond our grasp for a very long time; that it is a very hard problem indeed. The theme of artificial intelligence is pervasive in our fiction, from Star Trek's ship computer and the character Data, to the movie *Terminator.* Most laypersons (non computer-scientists) believe that powerful AI systems are just around the corner. In Professor Winograd's class, we learned that the human mind is far more marvelous than most of us can comprehend, and that true AI is still a long, long way off.

While writing my term paper for Winograd's class, I had one of those "Aha!" moments, and wrote my first paper on memes, in which I argued that AI could arise as an "emergent property" of the "meme complex" that comprised the computer-science community. My term paper's thesis was that a computer system was possible that was beyond the comprehension of any one individual computer scientist, that even though we as individuals weren't smart enough to create AI, it might be that the *memeplex* of computer science could *evolve* an AI system. In a nutshell, I realized that the rules Charles Darwin discovered that guide evolution in nature can be abstracted to a higher level, and applied to other domains.

Professor Winograd gave me a decent grade on the paper. I think he found my claims to be rather far fetched and fanciful (and he was right), but he gave me credit for the sheer originality and amusement value of my paper.

I was attending Stanford University thanks to a graduate-studies grant from the Hewlett Packard Company. Although I was grateful to HP for the grant, I was quickly becoming a disillusioned employee, having been hired during the unfortunate period right after Bill Hewlett and Dave Packard retired from their day-to-day management of the company's operations. Almost immediately after they retired, the company started an inexorable slide into ordinariness, to transform itself from a unique company that made you feel like part of a family, into just-another-Silicon-Valley-computermaker. It was a very sad time for me and many other HP employees, to watch something special slowly disappear.

As this downhill process continued at Hewlett Packard, I started thinking about memes and cultural evolution, and the paper I'd written for Professor Winograd's class. It struck me that memetics could give real insight into Hewlett Packard's changing culture. Silicon Valley corporations are evolving, competing entities that all share a single "ecosphere." They compete for the same employees, they produce similar goods, they sell to the same consumers, they pay the same taxes, and they buy from the same raw-material suppliers. They even dump their sewage down the same drains, which is a lot more important than you might think: It costs a small fortune to dispose of all of the toxic chemicals and heavy metals that Silicon Valley companies consume and discard.

I did a bit of exploratory writing about Hewlett Packard, corporate culture and memes, and quickly discovered that memetics gave amazing insights into virtually *all* aspects of human culture. My exploratory writings expanded and expanded, covering jokes, corporations, music, hunter/gatherer knowledge, literature ... and there was one brief chapter about religion. Then a new job, a move to a different state, the joy and hard work of raising three young children, and a dozen other events, took over, and without any conscious decision to do so, I put the book aside. But my fascination for the subject never waned, and I kept reading everything I could lay my hands on. Religion books, sociology books, meme books, history books, biographies of corporate presidents, on and on. Anything I could find that taught me more about the behavior of memes and memeplexes went into my pile of books to read.

That was two decades ago. During those two decades, much has happened: The word "meme" has entered the popular lexicon, and several excellent books have been published. The political and social climate in America has changed dramatically. There has been a "sea change," a dramatic shift in the winds, in the religious climate in America. Religious dialog has simultaneously become *both* more conservative *and* more liberal. On the conservative side, America's religious right has had a huge resurgence in power and influence. On the liberal side, several excellent books harshly critical of religion and religious dogma became bestsellers recently: David Mills' *Atheist Universe*, Bart Erman's *Misquoting Jesus*, Richard Dawkins' *The God Delusion*, Daniel Dennett's *Breaking the Spell*, Dan Barker's *Godless*, Sam Harris' *The End of Faith*, and Christopher Hitchens' *God is not Great*. While Erman is hardly an atheist, his carefully researched and very readable book opened the eyes of millions regarding the "inerrancy" of the Bible. David Mills' simple and readable arguments supporting the atheist view is hugely popular. Dawkins' direct and unapologetic rejection of religion seems harsh to many readers, but his book is thorough and well reasoned. Dennett takes a careful philosopher's approach, aiming in particular at American Christianity, to expose its hold on politics and daily lives. Barker tells the fascinating tale of an Evangelical Christian who became one of America's best-known atheists. And Hitchens makes the claim that religion "poisons everything," very strong words indeed. Just ten years ago, the socio-political climate in America would have made these books nearly impossible to publish; today they're on the shelves at the mega-stores.

The spark that brought this book back to life was my father's illness and death, and my conversations with Aunt Carolyn, the story of which is told as the final *Interlude*, below. The illness and death of someone close brings on an examination of ones' own life. My grandfather had seen religion as his salvation from his "misery," whereas my father, ironically, was just the opposite, blaming religion for much of what went wrong in his life. I thought they were both mistaken, focusing their energy on religion rather than on their own lives and their own actions. My grandfather used religion as an anesthetic, and my father used it as an excuse. I was pleased to find that I hadn't fallen into the same traps they had, of using religion to avoid responsibility for my own life. Whatever decisions I'd made, whatever directions my life had taken, those were *my* decisions. But why, I kept asking, had two intelligent, well-educated men fallen into the same trap, albeit in different ways?

That, ultimately, was what made me "put pen to paper" again: To answer that very question, both for my own personal satisfaction, and because I think it's an important message for all of humanity.

7. Why is Religion So Appealing?

How can it be, the non-believer asks, that in spite of all the advances we've made in physics, philosophy, biology, and chemistry, that people still cling to religions that were formed thousands of years ago? Why is religion is so incredibly tenacious? God's existence is completely unprovable, and has no foundation in science or logic. So why is God's existence so passionately believed by so many people?

Dogs and Cuckoo Birds

Since the whole affair had become one of religion, the vanquished were of course exterminated.
– Voltaire (1694-1778)

Can the International Red Cross save human lives by saving dogs? The answer to this question has surprising relevance to the question of the incredible tenacity of religion.

On Monday, October 22, 2007, my family and I awoke at dawn to the sound of a police bullhorn telling us to evacuate immediately. The *Witch Creek* wildfire was racing across San Diego County, and was almost at our doorstep. As quickly as we could, we gathered a few clothes, our three dogs and a cat, piled into our small Chevy RV, and drove toward the ocean, not knowing if we'd ever see our home again. We could see flames not a half mile away, and the sky was so dark with smoke that we had to turn on our headlights.

There were a few tragic deaths, including several heroic firefighters, but the mass evacuation of over 500,000 people was remarkably successful, and kept most people out of harm's way. I was among the fortunate – the firemen stopped the blaze just fifty meters from my house.

Now imagine you could replay that same scene: A frightening, wind-whipped wildfire approaching, police bullhorn blaring, smoke billowing across the neighborhood, a rush to pack our most precious things, but *the dogs and cat have to stay behind.* What would you do?

Emergency workers recently realized that many people think of their dogs and cats as full members of the family. Millions of Americans were heartsick at the sight of soggy, starving dogs on rooftops and tree branches in New Orleans after Hurricane Katrina. During the Witch Creek fire, one of my neighbors was despondent over a cat who ran out the door as they were evacuating, and had to be left behind. (The cat was later found safe.) When asked to abandon a pet, rescuers find that many people won't do it. They'll stay behind with their pets, risking injury and even death, rather than leave their beloved cats, dogs and horses to starve, drown or burn. By saving pets, emergency workers are able to save *more* human lives.

What is a Parasite?

Man is a dog's idea of what God should be.
– Holbrook Jackson

We're accustomed to living with dogs and cats, and we feel a strong bond with our pets, so it's hard to "step back" and see just how odd it is from nature's point of view. It is *highly* unusual for an animal (human or otherwise) to risk its life to protect a member of a different species. But its not completely unknown, except that in any other species, we'd quickly call it by its proper name: Parasitism.

When someone says the word "parasite," most of us think of leeches, tapeworms, fleas, and other unpleasant creatures. But parasites come in many forms, and use a variety of tricks to take advantage of the "host" species. The plague bacteria known as the Black Death killed nearly one third of the population in Europe in the mid-fourteenth century because of a special trick: It first attacks what immunologists call your spleen's "innate" immune cells and destroys them, leaving your body without its most important immune system.

Larger parasites such as tapeworms have evolved mechanisms that suppress your gut's natural immune reaction. Your body wants to get rid of them, but can't, because the tapeworm exudes chemicals that tell your body, "It's OK, there's nothing here to worry about."

These creepy creatures fit our normal notion of a parasite. But far more interesting are the *behavioral* parasites. Rather than tricking the biochemistry or immune system of their host, they *behave* in a way that tricks the host. The nest-parasite cuckoo birds are probably the best known examples of this sort of parasitism: They lay their eggs in the nest of other bird species. The egg is colored or speckled so that the host birds can't tell it from their own. When the baby cuckoo hatches, the "parent" birds are fooled by its appearance and behavior, and nurture it as they would their own. Often, the cuckoo chick will even kill the other chicks by pushing them out of the nest.

This "behavioral parasitism" works because the baby cuckoo looks and behaves enough like the parents' own chicks that they are fooled. There is no leech-like bloodsucking, or black-death spleen damage, or tapeworm immune suppression. It all happens through visual and audio cues: The parent birds think they are raising their own babies.

What is Natural Selection?

All of the ills from which America suffers can be traced to the teaching of evolution.
– William Jennings Bryan.

How did our dogs become the behavioral parasites on the human species?

"Survival of the fittest" is a remarkably flexible concept. When we learn about evolution, we study things like big teeth, sharp claws, faster feet, longer fur, and better camouflage – all traits that are important in the wild. It's easy to see that the rabbit who escapes from the coyote is "fitter" and can pass its genes on to its little rabbits. But what about a pet rabbit that *doesn't* escape from a human, because it has beautiful white fur, floppy ears, and big, lovable eyes?

Is that rabbit "more fit" than its brother rabbit with less snowy fur, smaller ears, and eyes that aren't quite as cute?

The answer is an emphatic *Yes!* Evolution *doesn't care* why a particular trait is more or less likely to lead to reproductive success. The word "nature" in "natural selection" seems to suggest that human activities don't count, but nothing could be farther from the truth. *Any* force that alters the survival of a gene is part of evolution.

My three dogs are the perfect example of this. When wolves took up residence with humans, our likes and dislikes started transforming the wild wolves into *canis lupus familiarus*, the familiar dog. In the wild, wolves have to catch their prey, survive bitter, cold winters, and compete with each other for mates. But once they hooked up with humans, the evolutionary forces changed dramatically. Humans provided most of the food, and built fires and houses to keep the dogs warm. The sharp teeth and warm winter coat were not as important as they used to be. But humans also introduced a new "fitness" criterion: Whether humans *liked* the dogs.

A wolf. Not cute.

Camping while evacuated from the Witch Creek Fire. Would you leave these three behind?

Take a look at the photos above. A wolf doesn't look cute, and even one that is raised as a pet never becomes very friendly. No amount of love or training can change a wolf into a lovable family pet. But Brisby, Skittles and Rocky are just about as lovable and cute as can be. Notice how they look childish compared to the wolf, especially their large, pretty eyes. And it's not just their looks; these three are an integral part of our family social life. They go on walks with us, watch TV with us, are fiercely protective when strangers knock, and know just how to give you "the look" when you're eating something they want. We don't just like our dogs, we *love* them.

These three small dogs together consume roughly a kilogram of quality food each day, high in protein and nutrients. The money I spend on these three cute parasites could easily support several families in impoverished countries.

Over the last 15,000 years, we humans have made this happen. We've done such an excellent job breeding for cute and friendly dogs that I'd trust my three dogs around a baby. Dogs that were friendlier, happier, cuter, and that fit into the human social hierarchy better, were more likely to be kept and nurtured by humans. Dogs that were dangerous, mean, ugly, or unfriendly were less fit, and were not as likely to be kept as pets.

It's easy for us to recognize parasitism in a cuckoo, because we're objective. But it's much harder for us to see that we are in a similar relationship with our pets. Dogs and cats appeal to our nurturing instincts – the instincts that tell us to feed and protect our own babies, and to seek out other humans as companions. Dogs and cats are behavioral parasites, acting as our *surrogate children and family,* satisfying our maternal/paternal instincts, just as the cuckoo chick makes its surrogate parents happy.

Why Is Religion So Appealing?

I have recently been examining all the known superstitions of the world, and do not find in our particular superstition (Christianity) one redeeming feature. They are all alike, founded on fables and mythology.
– Thomas Jefferson (1743-1826)

We started this chapter with the the non-believer's perplexing question: Why is religion so incredibly tenacious? Why is it still around, in spite of the advances of science, and the complete lack of any proof of God's existence?

Religion memes have been around for the 10,000 years of recorded human history, and certainly much longer than that, far back into prehistory. It is safe to say various forms of the religion virus have been around for at least 1,000 generations, and probably more like 10,000 generations or even more.

During those millennia, the many competing religion meme-plexes have constantly changed and evolved. In each generation, thousands of variants (mutations) competed against one another for "space" in the ideosphere – our collective brains. For example, today we have Hindus, Buddhists, Christians, Muslims, Jews (just to mention the world's major religions), and within each one there are many, many sects. Christians have two major divisions, Eastern and Western, and just within the Western there are Catholics, Lutherans, Methodist, Baptists, Protestants, and hundreds more. Jews and Muslims have an equally diverse list of variants, as do Buddhists and Hindus. The lists go on and on. That's a *lot* of competition, and a *lot* of variation, among the various versions of the Religion Virus.

All through recorded history, the ideosphere has been full of thousands and thousands of competing god-memes and religion memeplexes. We've already discussed the early history of religion, how simplistic human-like gods gave way to more powerful (and fewer) gods, and how that changed to monotheism. At each step, each one of the religion memes was competing against all the others other for attention, for retelling, for *believability*, and for *appeal*. Each meme "wanted" to be the one meme passed on to the next generation of the human ideosphere.

As a result of this evolutionary process, the religion memeplex evolved into a *behavioral parasite*. It has evolved to please us, to fit into an important place in our society, and in our wishes, desires, hopes and fears.

Think back to the baby cuckoo bird, whose "parents" are happy because their instincts tell them they're raising a fine young bird. And think back to my dogs, highly evolved to look young and cute, and to fit into my family in the same role as one of my own children – to *please me*. The Religion Virus has done the same thing: It has evolved to give us satisfying answers to some of life's most perplexing mysteries, to make us happy. But unlike my dogs, the Religion Virus also has a darker side, in that it also works through our fears. It also *scares* us into believing it.

Nature, that is, evolution, has equipped us with hunger and sexual desire, to ensure that we feed ourselves and mate. It has equipped us with pain and fear, so that we will avoid injury and danger. It has equipped us with jealousy so that we keep others from our mates, with xenophobia so that we're wary of strangers, and with a deep love for our children so that we'll protect them until they grow up and have children of their own.

The Religion Virus has evolved to fit perfectly into our hopes, fears, hunger, lust, jealousy, xenophobia, and parental love, to hijack these instincts for its own survival. It gives us hope when there is none. It tells us that when bad things happen, there is a reason, and there is a reward that will come our way if keep our faith. It tells us that those who harm us will get their punishment, if not in this life, then in the next one. It tells us that death is not final, that it is merely the start of something even better. It tells us that our children are going to be punished with eternal damnation if we don't pass the virus to them. The list goes on and on, including the main memes we've studied so far, and a host of others. And *the truth of these beliefs is irrelevant.* "When you die, you're dead and gone," isn't nearly as attractive as, "When you die, you'll live on forever in eternal joy," regardless of which one is true. The Religion Virus today is made of the memes that we really, really *want* to believe.

Each Religion Virus today is the result of ten thousand generations of competition with other Religion Viruses, and only the best survived. Your parents taught you their religion because it was the *most believable* to them, and the religion your parents learned from your grandparents was the variant your grandparents found most believable, and so on back through history. The religion virus that infected you is the one that was the best at each generation, the most attractive, the *survivor*. At each point in history, it out-competed the other ideas, to be carried down to you. The survivors were the ideas that fit the very best into the human mind, that were the best at manipulating both our hopes, desires, dislikes and fears.

The Religion Virus is good at infecting your brain. It's damned good, because if it wasn't, some *other* memeplex would be the one you believed in.

Why Start so Young?

Give me the boy, and I'll give you the man.
– Saint Ignatius of Loyola (1491-1556)

One particular aspect of the Religion Virus' evolution is so important that it deserves special attention: The need to teach religion to children, while they are still impressionable.

One story that illustrates this point is from a wartime letter by Arthur Evelyn Waugh regarding his close friend, Randolph Churchill (son of Sir Winston Churchill), when Churchill and Waugh were officers serving together in World War II. Churchill had somehow managed to become an adult without ever reading the Bible or being exposed in a serious way to Christian theology. He kept going on about it, until Waugh got exasperated. He wrote:

In the hope of keeping him quiet for a few hours Freddy & I have bet Randolph 20 [pounds sterling] that he cannot read the whole Bible in a fortnight. It would have been worth it at the price. Unhappily it has not had the result we hoped. He has never read any of it before and is hideously excited; keeps reading quotations aloud 'I say I bet you didn't know this came in the Bible "bring down my grey hairs in sorrow to the grave"' or merely slapping his side & chortling 'God, isn't God a sh**!'
– A. Evelyn Waugh, letter to Nancy Mitford, November of 1944

In our chapter about human language, we noted that for memes to be passed reliably from generation to generation, the human brain has to be open to absorbing vast quantities of knowledge and information during youth, and then as the human reaches adulthood, the brain must "solidify" its beliefs so that the information will be passed accurately to the next generation of children. Most of our deeply held beliefs and culturally acquired behaviors must therefore be taught to our children. By the time we're adults, it's too late.

The Religion Virus, like any other evolving entity, has adapted to fit its environment. As its evolution proceeded down through the millennia, religious memeplexes that *didn't* emphasize the religious education of children were far less likely to be stable, to resist mutation. On the other hand, religious memeplexes that included strong memes for teaching children were far more likely to survive and propagate.

This is readily seen in the fact that all of the major religions begin teaching children at a *very* young age. Children are taught their bedtime prayers almost as soon as they can talk. Houses of worship, whether Christian, Jewish, Muslim, Buddhist or Hindi, all include special classrooms for toddlers, children, and teenagers. And just as significant, children of atheists are *far* more likely to be atheists, since they too were taught their atheistic beliefs starting from a young age, mostly by the *lack* of any training in religion.

Interlude: A Cough that can Kill

*As a well-spent day brings happy sleep, so a life well used
brings a happy death.*
– Leonardo da Vinci

The state of New Mexico, in America's Southwest, is a fascinating place, one of the few places in America with a large Hispanic
population of people who are *not* recent immigrants. Many New
Mexicans trace their family back over 400 years or more, to the time
of the first Spanish settlements, and are farming the lands that were
farmed by their fathers, grandfathers and many more generations.
The Pueblo Indians of New Mexico are also unique in America as
the only Native Americans who never had their land stolen and then
returned in the form of "Indian reservations." They've lived on their
own land continuously since time immemorial.

This long, rich tradition of family life and strong communities,
combined with the incredible natural beauty of the mountains of
northern New Mexico, made it a wonderful place to live and raise
my children. I had the good fortune to live in Santa Fe, New Mexico
for six years.

One of the unfortunate side effects of living side-by-side with
Indian culture is the number of slightly nutty spiritual groups who
are attracted to the Native Americans' religion and culture. Among
non-Indians in America, the Indians have developed a sort of mys-
tique, of being more connected to the Earth, to nature, and to the
spirit world. Many non-Indians envy what they see as a higher level
of spiritual purity, simplicity, and morality that goes along with the
Indian heritage.

In addition to this attraction that religious seekers feel for the
Indian religion, they're also drawn to the beautiful, majestic mountains of New Mexico that soar to 4,500 meters and more, and believe
that by connecting directly with the bedrock granite that is the
"bones" of the Earth, and by ascending to the great heights, they may

gain more insight or even connect to the earthly spirits that reside in those mountains.

Which is a long way of explaining that northern New Mexico is dotted with any number of small groups of recent immigrants, almost all of them "Anglo," who moved there and formed small religious communities, each with its own unique and/or peculiar brand of spirituality. (The term "Anglo" is used by New Mexicans to describe everyone who is not Hispanic. Even the African-American sheriff who was elected one year was an Anglo by the New Mexico reckoning, which he found quite amusing!).

The last year that I lived in New Mexico, I got a cough. At first it seemed like a normal cold or influenza coming on, but not for long. Within a day or two it was clear that this was no ordinary cough. It was like nothing I'd ever had before (or since). Huge, deep, wracking coughs, accompanied by intense pain, that went on and on and on. The cough was so severe that I pulled my diaphragm muscles from the exertion, which, since the cough went unabated, just added to my misery. I'll spare you the details of doctor visits, whole quarts of codeine cough syrup, and having to stay in the guest room so that the rest of the family could at least get some rest, but the entire ordeal lasted over six weeks, and my throat never fully recovered.

You can imagine my surprise when the doctor diagnosed it as whooping cough! I thought whooping cough was eradicated in America, that it was a thing of the past. But no, it still pops up here and there. And it's almost exclusively a disease of religious sects whose members refuse to let their children be immunized against childhood diseases. It turned out there was a small epidemic in Santa Fe, caused by some of the aforementioned religious sects. Along with embracing Indian spirituality, these people also reject modern medicine and immunizations, and their children were vulnerable.

Epidemiologists have a term they call "herd immunity." Suppose you have 10,000 cattle, and 9,998 of these cows are immunized against a disease. Now imagine one of the two remaining cows gets sick – what are the chances that the second cow will catch the disease from the first cow? Probably very low. The two cows, the sick one and the unimmunized one, will each come in contact with a few dozen or hundred cows every day, but the chances that they'll bump into each other before the sick cow recovers are not that good. So the sick cow will probably get better, the unimmunized cow will never get sick, and the disease will come to a dead end in that herd.

In essence, the *herd's immunity* protects the unimmunized cow. The other cows act like a barrier that the disease can't cross to get to the one vulnerable cow.

Now imagine instead that 100 of the cows are not immunized, and one of those 100 gets sick. Since 1% of the cows are susceptible, the chances are pretty good that, in the few days during which the sick cow is infectious, she will bump into an unimmunized cow or two, and those cows will get sick. Then they'll bump into other unimmunized cows ... and pretty soon all 100 of the unimmunized cows will get sick.

In other words, it only takes a small percentage of a population to be vulnerable for the "herd immunity" to disappear. And that's exactly what happened with whooping cough in New Mexico. As more and more of these anti-immunization groups moved into the state, and their children started attending public schools, their numbers passed above the threshold at which the herd immunity disappears. When one student got sick – perhaps by visiting another state or country – and went to school, the disease rapidly spread to most of the unimmunized students.

Unfortunately for me, I also learned that the childhood immunizations we all got against whooping cough don't always last forever; sometimes the immunity wears off after only 20-40 years. So I became a victim of these religious luddites. In case you've never had whooping cough, you're not missing anything. I used to wonder how anyone could die just from coughing, but now I know.

8. The Atheist's Paradox

The Paradox

> *A physician is not angry at the intemperance of a mad patient, nor does he take it ill to be railed at by a man in a fever. Just so should a wise man treat all mankind, as a physician treats a patient, and look upon them only as sick and extravagant.*
> *– Lucius Annaeus Seneca (4 BC - AD 65)*

Atheists might be roughly divided into two groups: The "Live and Let Live Atheists," who feel religion is misguided but harmless, and the "Anti-Religion Atheists," who believe religion is harmful. Some strongly anti-religion atheists even claim that religion is at the root of most of the world's evil, and assert that without religion, peace would reign and poverty and disease could be eliminated. Several bestselling books criticizing religion include words like "poison" and "delusion" in their titles.

These strong anti-religion views are not typical of atheists, but it is fair to say many or most atheists believe that religion does more harm than good. At the same time, almost all atheists believe in Darwin's Evolution Science.

These two beliefs, in Darwin's evolution and that religion is harmful, seem to create a paradox. The Christian satirist Becky Garrison, who gets many things wrong, is at least a good writer. Garrison puts the paradox succinctly, and shows that this is a genuine problem that atheists need to address. She writes:

> *Here's a real puzzler to hard-core Darwinians. If religion were a truly useless and destructive mechanism with no redemptive quantities whatsoever, then wouldn't faith be extinct by now? At the very least, I expect religion would be akin to an appendix or tonsils. ... [W]hat does this say to us, that religion is still standing?*

As we've seen many times, evolution has a harsh and effective way of filtering out traits that are harmful. If religion is so awful, why hasn't evolution changed the human brain to make it resistant to religious memes? This is the anti-religion atheist's paradox: Why hasn't evolution turned us all into atheists?

There are two errors in Garrison's conclusion.

First, Garrison makes a classic mistake about evolution: Natural Selection works on the *individual*, not the group. Religion is an individual choice, but the burdens of religion may be on *society*. If religious beliefs benefits the individual, natural selection will favor it, even if religion is bad for society as a whole.

Second, parasites and symbiotes are *very* common in nature. Just because something is harmful doesn't mean you can get rid of it.

Let's explore these points in some detail, and see how they resolve the paradox.

The Tragedy of the Commons

> *It ain't those parts of the Bible that I can't understand that bother me, it's the parts that I do understand.*
> *– Mark Twain (1835-1910)*

The difference between what's good for the individual and how that can be radically different from what's good for society is illustrated by the classic 1968 paper by zoologist Garrett Hardins entitled *The Tragedy of the Commons*. Imagine a village with ten farmers, and a pasture that the farmers all share ("the commons"), which can support about one hundred cows before overgrazing starts to damage the pasture. Good sense tells us that the if the farmers want to maximize the village's income, and be fair to everyone, then each farmer should have ten cows.

But good sense for the village is *not* good sense for each farmer – it's an inherently unstable situation. Suppose one greedy farmer buys an eleventh cow, what happens? The pasture now has 101 cows, which isn't really all that much different than 100, maybe the grass is a *little* degraded, and the overall herd productivity is a *little* less. But the greedy farmer fares quite well, his productivity is up almost ten percent!

In other words, each individual farmer is motivated to do something that's bad for the village. The cost of the extra cow is shared by all ten farmers, but the benefit goes to the one "greedy" farmer. If the village sticks to one hundred cows, the total weight of the herd (all the cows' weight combined) will be maximized. But if any individual farmer breaks the rules and buys an eleventh cow, *that farmer* will make more money.

The real tragedy that ensues is when the other nine farmers each look at the situation, and logically conclude that they should also each buy another cow. "After all," a farmer might say, "why should I be the only farmer with just ten cows?" So they too buy an extra cow, and now the pasture is seriously overgrazed. Perhaps one of the farmers, disappointed that his production isn't what he hoped for, buys a twelfth cow ... and so forth. The farmers' individual decisions are all logical, almost inevitable, yet the result is that all of the farmers are worse off than if they'd stuck with ten cows to begin with.

This is the "tragedy of the commons." In any situation where there is a commons, a shared resource, the economic forces almost guarantee the destruction of the commons. Whether it's a pasture for a few farmers, or the Pacific Ocean salmon fisheries, the individual is motivated to overuse the resource, to the detriment of all. The farmer buys too many cows, the fisherman catches too many fish, and the net result is disastrous.

This "tragedy of the commons" happens all the time in evolution. Recall from our earlier chapters that most species have far more offspring than can possibly survive, whether it's a spider laying thousands of eggs, a rabbit having dozens or hundreds of baby rabbits, or a mushroom spewing millions of spores into the air.

Rabbits' breeding habits are almost an exact analogy to the farmers-and-cows story. In any given ecology, the food available to the rabbits is limited, and there is some number of rabbits that would be best in that given ecology. Fewer rabbits, and some of the food goes to waste, more rabbits, and they start to starve, and to degrade their environment.

But do the rabbits breed until they get to this optimal population and then stop? No! They keep "breeding like rabbits." Rabbits that have the most babies are the ones whose genes get passed on to the next generation. If there was some sort of "responsibility gene" that told certain rabbits to slow down when the food ran short, the rabbits that *didn't* have that gene would breed faster, and the "responsibility gene" would quickly disappear. The brutal and inexorable "survival of the fittest" guarantees that the rabbits will breed far beyond the optimal population.

The idea of a "responsibility gene" in rabbits is amusing, but it has a real counterpart in the ideosphere of human memes: The *Zero Population Growth (ZPG) Meme*. In 1968, entomologist Paul Erlich published a seminal book called *The Population Bomb*, in which he pointed out that without family planning worldwide, humanity was facing a population "explosion" that could only end in famine, starvation, and probably wars. Erlich's book had some mathematical errors that made his predictions overly pessimistic, but he nevertheless brought the topic of zero population growth into the mainstream of modern thinking.

The idea that responsible families should limit themselves to two children, or even fewer, became a new ethic in America and Europe. Prior to Erlich's book, couples who had three, four, five or even more children were congratulated, but by the mid-1970's, large families were considered in many social circles to be a sign of irresponsibility. The *ZPG Meme* was firmly planted in American and European culture.

Just four short decades later, evolution has already started shredding the *ZPG Meme*. In countries like Germany, France, Switzerland, and The Netherlands, immigrants from places like Turkey, Africa, and the Middle East, people who never acquired the *ZPG Meme,* still have a very high birth rate. The native Germans, whose birth rate is *below* replacement levels, are facing a future where they will be the minority in their own country within a decade or two, overwhelmed by immigrant Germans who don't believe in the *ZPG Meme* and continue to have lots of children. The *ZPG Meme* is thus breeding itself out of existence.

Getting back to the point that started this chapter: Becky Garrison asked the question: If religion is so bad, why hasn't evolution eliminated it? We now know there is at least one scientific explanation: "Survival of the fittest" works on individuals, not on species or societies, whether we're talking about genetic evolution or memetic evolution. It is entirely possible for something to be harmful to the species, or to society, yet still be favored by evolution.

Parasites, Hitchhikers, and Symbiotes

Man is certainly stark mad; he cannot make a flea, yet he makes gods by the dozens.
– Michel De Montaigne

The coral reefs and small islands that make up the South Pacific Kwajalein Atoll are among the most beautiful in the world. Like a string of pearls, they encircle one of the world's largest oceanic lagoons, over 2,000 square kilometers in the Marshall Islands of Micronesia. The first occupants arrived in the area over 3,000 years ago, and lived in relative obscurity until World War II. Sadly, their ancient way of life came to an abrupt end when the Japanese and Americans fought fierce battles on Kwajalein Island.

The real destruction of their ancient ways of living didn't start until a few years later when the United States decided to use the Kwajalein Atoll as the target area for intercontinental ballistic missiles and ballistic missile interceptors. Missiles were aimed at Kwajalein, and the interceptors tried to blow them up before they arrived. Needless to say, the United States couldn't have a bunch of people living in the target area, so the Islanders were uprooted from their ancient home islands. The tiny island of Ebeye at the south end of the atoll was virtually paved over, and a small city was built. Something like 6,000 Islanders were taken from their rich fishing grounds and coconut groves, and packed into the tiny island.

The Kwajalein Islanders, for a time at least, had a remarkably low incidence of suicide, in spite of the massive overcrowding on the island, and the culture shock caused by the United States' policies. For ten years, from 1955 to 1965, there wasn't a *single* suicide on the entire island of Ebeye. In 1966, a young man in jail hanged himself, but the event had little impact. Then, a few months later, another young man, the popular and respected son of a prominent businessman, found himself with two lovers and a baby by each. Despondent over his situation, he killed himself to avoid facing the consequences.

Three weeks later, another young man killed himself in a "copycat" suicide, then another, and the toll started mounting. In the next ten years, there were twenty-five suicides, all very similar to one another. It was almost always young men, almost always by hanging, and almost always accompanied by a note similar to the one written by the young man who started it all. The act of suicide gained a sort of cult underground status in the communities, and was found in graffiti, on T-shirts, and in the words of local songs played on the radio.

The "Micronesian Suicide meme" is best understood as a "disease germ," an idea that is inherently harmful, yet "sticks" because it has other traits that make it fascinating or appealing. Suicide and death have a dark attraction for teenagers who are maturing and learning the reality of their own mortality.

We've discussed both ends of the spectrum of inter-species relationships, from symbiosis (beneficial to both species) to fatal diseases (bad for both species). In reality, the relationships between species cover the whole spectrum, from diseases and parasites, to species so symbiotically intertwined that neither can live without the other.

You might be surprised to find that disease-causing organism are the *least* common infection in your body. Most of the critters that live in and on you cause few or no symptoms at all. These organisms' strategies are much more successful than a disease-causing infection. They slip in unnoticed, usually early in your life, and find their niche, perhaps on your skin, your eyelashes, your hair, or your gut.

Eye mites (*demodex folliculorum* or demodicids) are a great example. Most of us have these little worm-like mites living in the roots of our eyelashes. They're only 0.4 mm long (about fifteen thousandths of an inch), so they're essentially invisible, and the worst they'll ever do is make your eyes itch a little. You may have as many as a dozen or more on each of your eyelashes, yet most of us don't even know (or want to know) they're there.

Notice how the eye mite's successful strategy contrasts with disease-causing species. An influenza virus faces a hostile, and ultimately fatal, environment in your body. It has just a week or two to reproduce, make you sneeze and cough to infect the next person, before your body kills it off completely. It's tough being an influenza virus. By contrast, the eye mite settles in for the duration. An eye mite and its descendants will be with you, living peacefully and undisturbed, for your entire life.

Memes have a similar spectrum of relationships with humans. Some are symbiotic, in that they help you stay safe, find food, attract a mate, enjoy life, reproduce, and live comfortably. A meme in a hunter-gatherer tribe might help the tribe remember where certain foods can be found at different times of the year. Joke memes are fun and help us to relax and enjoy life. Morality memes help us get along and behave well towards one another. The meme that says, "Save the women and children" helps protect our families.

But, as in the biological world, there are parasitic memes, ideas that are harmful, yet survive. Memes that encourage young men to join gangs, encourage tobacco use, encourage credit-card overspending, and encourage drug use, are all harmful. Yet they thrive in our modern societies, and are remarkably hard to eradicate.

Alien Invaders

Everyone is quick to blame the alien.
Aeschylus (525-456 BC)

In October of 1859, Mr. Thomas Austin, of Winchelsea, Victoria (Australia) started one of the worst scourges in modern history. Mr. Austin managed to wipe out one eighth of all mammalian species in the entire continent of Australia, and the plant life across the continent was devastated so badly we can't calculate the full extent. Mr. Austin started a severe erosion problem that continue to this day, sweeping vast swaths of Australia's fertile topsoil out to sea. The damage Mr. Austin caused to Australian agriculture, ecosystem and economy is incalculable.

What horrible crime did Mr. Thomas Austin commit? On that fateful October day of 1859, Mr. Austin turned twenty-four rabbits loose. He was an avid hunter, and he missed the good ol' days back in England where he could go out and bag a few rabbits for his dinner table. So he wrote to his nephew to send along a few rabbits (along with some hares, partridges and sparrows).

Unfortunately, Australia proved a test case for the old saying, "They're breeding like rabbits." Within a mere ten years, those twenty-four rabbits had proliferated so much that over *two million* could be killed every year without making a dent in their population. Today, their destructive habits continue unabated, costing the farmers and government of Australia hundreds of millions of dollars each year in rabbit-abatement, damage to crops and other problems that they cause. They've even managed to survive the deliberate introduction of two rabbit plagues, a deadly *myxoma* virus which the government introduced in 1950, and a less effective *calcivirus* (Rabbit Hemorrhagic Disease) in 1996.

On the major continents, species have a hard life. Virtually every plant, animal, insect, and fungus competes fiercely for its "supper" (whatever that might be), and is constantly battling predators and parasites. Grass gets eaten by rabbits, rabbits get eaten by coyotes, and coyotes are plagued by fleas and ticks, plus they must outsmart the wolves, bobcats and cougars who also want to eat rabbits. Nobody has "the good life."

One of the more fascinating consequences of the principles of evolution is that species tend to "coevolve" in a way that keeps species balanced. Imagine, for example, that the coyotes somehow evolved to be much faster than rabbits, so that they could easily catch all the rabbits they wanted. Sounds great (for the coyotes), right? Wrong – the coyotes would quickly kill all of the rabbits, then the coyotes would starve and become extinct.

Suppose instead that rabbits evolved to be much faster than coyotes, so that they'd never be caught. Sounds grand (for the rabbits), right? Wrong again. Faster rabbits have bigger muscles and bones, and it means these super-rabbits have to eat more to stay alive. Once the coyote population dwindled, the super-rabbits would be at an evolutionary *disadvantage*, because they would have to eat more to support the (now unnecessary) bones and muscles, so the lesser (slower) rabbits would have the advantage. Evolution constantly favors a *balance* between a huge variety of factors.

One of the most exciting synergies between two academic fields of study occurred when economists applied their mathematics to the field of evolution. The economists realized they could study ecosystems using a cost/benefit analysis. By weighing a benefit (a rabbit doesn't become a coyote's dinner) against a cost (the rabbit has to eat a more to support bigger muscles), economists were able to show why species tend to stay in a constant, balanced battle. If the rabbits get a little faster, the coyotes do too, but there's never a huge imbalance.

We already saw this effect in the previous section, where we noted that an infectious disease will die out if it is too deadly. If we look at this phenomenon from an economist's point of view, it makes perfect sense: The disease-causing organism gets benefits from invading your body (it can reproduce itself dramatically), but at the cost of possibly killing you. The ideal disease balances the costs and benefits, keeping you alive (but possibly altering your behavior) long enough for it to reproduce in the next victim.

When Mr. Austin's rabbits found themselves free in the Australian continent, all of the forces that had kept them in check were gone: There were no predators, no freezing winters, and none of the diseases that cut their numbers. And all the things that helped them thrive were easily available: Food was bountiful, the terrain was ideal, and by 1859 farming was widespread, giving the rabbits even more to eat. The rabbit's habit of breeding, well, like rabbits, was necessary in Europe because most rabbits died before reaching breeding age. But in Australia, most rabbits lived to maturity, and their population grew exponentially.

To be fair to Mr. Thomas Austin, terms like "ecology" and "evolution" were unknown in his day. Charles Darwin published his brilliant *Origin of the Species* in that same year, 1859, and it's a good bet that neither Mr. Austin or anyone else in Australia could have predicted dire consequences of releasing those rabbits. (Although Darwin himself, and many other scientists, had already documented the catastrophic effects that alien species can have.) Moreover, if Mr. Austin hadn't released the rabbits, someone else surely would have. Mr. Austin just happened to be the one history recorded as the perpetrator of this ecological catastrophe.

The story of rabbits in Australia is just one of the thousands of incidents of an "alien" (non-native) species that is introduced, causing untold ecological damage. The Mediterranean Fruit Fly destroyed the once-bountiful Hawai'ian fruit crops, while the tropical *caulerpa* algae is destroying the entire ecosystem of the Mediterranean Sea. Zebra mussels from Russian lakes are taking over America's Great Lakes. Water hyacinth from the Amazon River are suffocating fish and destroying water quality in Africa, costing African governments hundreds of millions of dollars per year. The list is distressingly long.

Culture and society are subject to the forces of evolution, just like rabbits and coyotes, as we've seen through our study of memes. Memes mutate, compete, and reproduce. It should be no surprise to find that there are "invasive alien species" in the world of memes, just like the rabbits of Australia. When a "foreign" meme is suddenly introduced into a culture, it can be just as devastating to the culture's established memes as the rabbits were to Australia's ecology.

The specific memeplex that interests us is, of course, religion. Consider the start of the seventeenth century, when the colonialist expansion period gained serious momentum. All of the major European powers were using their technological superiority to conquer and subjugate the rest of the world, primarily for economic gain. Along with the political and economic dominance came European religions – that is, Christianity.

The various Christian churches had been shaped and sharpened by sixteen centuries of inter- and intra-faith competition between the memes that make up the Christian religion viruses. And the memeplex didn't start with Jesus – we have studied extensively how the god Yahweh evolved and changed over thousands of years prior to the start of Christianity, and how even before Yahweh the religion memes were evolving. The competition among the various religious memes was fierce, and only the best, the ones that were the most appealing and had the best ability to reproduce, survived. Christianity was a highly evolved set of memes, filtered and improved by ten thousand or more years of the harshest meme competition in the history of the world.

The aboriginal religions of places like the Pacific Islands, Australia and New Zealand never had a chance. Although their religions were old, and were venerated by their people, they simply didn't have the "sharp teeth and claws" of the highly evolved Christian religion's memes. They weren't as fit. The concepts of heaven, hell, guilt, intolerance and all the others we've discussed, were fully mature by the seventeenth century, and they made short work of the local religion memes.

Sickle-Cell Anemia – Taking the Good with the Bad

The further the spiritual evolution of mankind advances, the more certain it seems to me that the path to genuine religiosity does not lie through the fear of life, and the fear of death, and blind faith, but through striving after rational knowledge.
– Albert Einstein (1879-1955)

Walter Clement Noel, a Caribbean man of African descent, was born on the island of Grenada in 1884. Because of changing race relations in the United States, blacks could be accepted at some universities and professional schools, although it was rare. Noel was an exceptional young man from a well-to-do Barbados family, with a solid education. His dream was realized when he was accepted at the Chicago College of Dental Surgery in 1904.

Unfortunately, before he even arrived in the United States, Mr. Noel already had serious health problems. He had bad skin lesions, joint pain, and shortness of breath. Not long after reaching Chicago, he was admitted to Presbyterian Hospital, where Dr. Ernest E. Irons, a twenty-seven-year-old intern working under the direction of Professor James B. Herrick, discovered something quite odd about Noel's blood – he had "peculiar elongated and sickle shaped" red blood cells. Over the next three years, Noel was readmitted to Presbyterian Hospital several times suffering from "muscular rheumatism" and "bilious attacks."

Walter Clement Noel graduated from dental school in 1907, and settled in Grenada where he became the second professionally trained dentist to practice in the capital city of St. Georges. But for Noel, like many others of African descent, his life was all too short. He practiced dentistry for the next nine years, but his symptoms persisted and worsened. Noel, the "first sickle cell anemia patient" died in 1916 at the age of thirty-two. Although his cause of death was listed as pneumonia, doctors today who are familiar with sickle cell anemia are virtually certain it was undetected pulmonary hypertension, caused by his disease.

Sickle cell anemia presented a paradox to scientists. The disease was well known to sub-Saharan Africans long before western medicine treated Walter Clement Noel. The Africans knew that it ran in families, and doctors who studied sickle cell anemia quickly learned that it was a genetic disease. Scientists and evolutionists were perplexed: Normally, a genetic disease that kills people such as Walter Clement Noel at a young age, and causes such severe illness, would quickly be eliminated by the inexorable filtering of natural selection. So why was sickle cell anemia so prevalent among the sub-Saharan Africans?

It turns out that in addition to its fatal effects, the deformed sickle-shaped red-blood cells are resistant to malaria. Malaria is widespread in the tropics, and particularly in the sub-Saharan Africa where sickle-cell anemia is common. When researchers put these two facts together, the "paradox" of sickle cell anemia was solved. The genetic disease was both harmful and beneficial, but the beneficial effects only help where malaria is common. Even though sickle cell anemia kills many people, *more are saved* by their resistance to malaria.

In other words, a genetic trait can be good *and* bad at the same time; the gene's survival depends on the net effect, not on just the good or the bad. Sickle cell anemia is only useful where malaria is present, and even there, the price of protection from malaria is paid for by much suffering and early death.

The Solution to The Atheist's Paradox

Two paradoxes are better than one; they may even suggest a solution.
– Edward Teller

The evolution of language, of your ability to receive memes from others and pass them on, had nothing to do with religion; language and memes evolved because they were hugely important to our survival and adaptability. But just as a virus can hijack the cells of your body to reproduce itself, human language can be hijacked for a different purpose by a "virus," in this case, the Religion Virus. The influenza virus doesn't "care" how or why all that cool biochemistry in your body's cells came into existence, it just uses it. Likewise, the Religion Virus doesn't care how human language came into existence, it just hijacks it for its own reproduction.

In this chapter, we learned that there are several reasons why harmful genes, and harmful memes, are not necessarily filtered out by evolution.

- If a meme benefits the individual, it will survive, even if it harms society as a whole (the "tragedy of the commons").
- Parasitic memes can hijack mechanisms (our ability to speak) that evolved for a different purpose.
- "Alien" memes can evolve in one culture, then as humans explore new regions, "invade" other cultures where they run rampant and exterminate the existing memes.
- Memes that have both good and bad aspects can survive, as long as the good outweighs the bad (like sickle cell anemia).

These four evolutionary principles are the solution to the atheist's paradox. Even though religion may be a net burden on society, this does *not* necessarily guarantee that evolution will filter it out. Our ability to speak, to pass memes from one generation to the next, gives us a huge evolutionary advantage over all other creatures on earth. When weighed against that, the religion virus could indeed be detrimental to society, and still survive.

The satirist Becky Garrison and her ilk, who try to turn Evolution Science against itself to "prove" that religion must be beneficial to humans, simply aren't educated enough in the beautiful and subtle details of Darwin's Evolution Science.

Interlude: Shakespeare, Genesis and the Big Bang

William Shakespeare didn't write all those plays. It was someone else with the same name.
– An old philosopher's joke

My youngest son's friend "Dale" (not his real name) has the strangest rationalization of the Biblical Genesis I've ever heard. Dale has the misfortune to be intelligent, inquisitive, and a fundamentalist Christian who believes the Bible is literally true. God, according to Dale, created the world six thousand years ago. But Dale is smart and *also* realizes that the evidence plainly shows that the Earth is over four billion years old, and that evolution is real.

These two beliefs are completely incompatible. So, according to Dale, for some inscrutable reason, God set everything up so that the universe looked *exactly* like it would if the "Big Bang" happened billions of years ago. Even though the stars are millions of light years away, God carefully placed photons headed for Earth so that it would *look* like the stars had been there all along. God carefully put fossils in the ground, and carved out rivers and mountains and valleys, all so that it would *appear* that Earth is billions of years old. God created all the plants, animals, fungus and other life forms *exactly* like they would have been if they'd evolved according to Darwin's principals of Evolution.

I was amazed to hear an otherwise rational, intelligent young man stretch so far to reconcile the facts about the world with his religious beliefs. The problem with his theory is that it's completely useless. I could just as well say that there are little green men living inside the sun, and assert (correctly) that you can't prove me wrong. The little-green-men hypothesis isn't right or wrong, it is *useless*. It's uninformative, unpredictive, and doesn't explain anything.

Dale's theory is not right or wrong, it is simply irrelevant. Dale claims God did this trick six thousand years ago, but I could just as well claim that God created the world yesterday, that we've only been on Earth for twenty-four hours, that God implanted all of our memories so that we'd think we'd been here all our lives. Dale couldn't prove me wrong. It's a modern-day analog of *solipsism*, which (very roughly speaking) asserts that we can't even prove that we even exist, so all other argument is useless.

I call it *sloppyism*, using unprovable, specious logic to divert intelligent people from real intellectual progress. Dale has discovered the same problem that bogged down some of the greatest philosophers of all time, including Emmanuel Kant. Kant was perplexed by the fact that a solipsist could assert, "The entire world is nothing more than my imagination, and you can't prove to me that you even exist other than in my mind." Kant famously called this, "the scandal of philosophy" that such a basic question as the existence of the world couldn't be answered. But the great German philosopher Martin Heidegger put it best:

> The 'scandal of philosophy' is not that [a proof for the existence of the world] has yet to be given, but that such proofs are expected and attempted again and again.
> – Being and Time (1927), Martin Heidegger

Dale needs to learn from Heidegger: The real scandal is making unprovable assertions to divert attention from important problems. Dale is trying to hold two irreconcilable truths, and to make it work, he invented an irrefutable bit of "logic." Unfortunately for Dale, and perhaps for the rest of us who will lose this bright young man's mind to the prison of religious rationalization, his strange explanation does nothing useful other than to rid Dale of his anxiety. Instead of furthering his quest for knowledge, Dale is now stuck on an intellectual dead-end street.

9. Religion, Technology
and Government

In the world of plants and animals, it often happens that some external force intervenes, altering the balance of a particular ecosystem to favor or harm species. A flood or drought can suddenly alter an ecosystem to favor one species over another. An ice age can lower the ocean's level, creating land bridges that suddenly (on the geological time scale) allow new species to invade a formerly isolated island, or even a whole continent. An asteroid can wipe out a large fraction of the large animals on Earth.

This book is primarily about memes and evolution, and how religion came into existence and evolved via the forces of natural selection. But cultural evolution doesn't happen in isolation. In this chapter, we're going to take a slight detour from our main topic, and examine some of the other forces that have influenced the development of the Religion Virus.

Cargo Cults

Any sufficiently advanced technology is indistinguishable from magic.
– Arthur C. Clarke

Imagine you are a forty-year-old South Pacific Islander, and the year is 1944. You are an expert fisherman, you know the ways of the sea, and you can navigate your *proa* (outrigger sailing canoe) across 500 miles of open ocean with nothing more than the wind, stars, birds and waves for navigation, just to visit your friends on the next island. You have children and grandchildren, and as an elder in your village, and a fine fisherman, you are enjoying the respect of the entire island. You are a well educated, skilled and experienced man, one who has accomplished everything a man could hope for.

One day a strange *proa*, bigger than yours and with no sail at all, comes to your island. Out of it come a half-dozen men, all dressed in strange clothing, and carrying many strange and wonderful objects. You've seen white men before, and heard stories from your neighboring islands, but never before have they come in such numbers, and stayed so long.

One of them speaks a few words of your language, enough that you can learn a bit of what they're doing. It seems they are in a war with some other tribe, one that lives far away. Although these men are strange, you understand warfare. These men tell you they're setting up a "radio", and explains that the tall tower, with long thin ropes that he calls "wires", will call down goods from the sky. You and your friends all find this very amusing, and wonder how these strange, crazy men are going to survive when they don't even know how to fish, and have no women with them.

But then, it happens! Strange, noisy machines fly overhead, like great birds, and the when these strange men speak their unknown language into their radio, these flying machines drop Cargo onto your island. And what Cargo! Food, blankets, guns, tents, and more machines! These men are rich beyond comprehension. Knives, axes and saws made of steel, sharper than anything you've dreamed of. Food that comes from cans and boxes, and these strange men never go fishing or climb the trees for coconuts or fruit. Machines that roll around your island at high speed with nobody pushing.

And then, one of your grandchildren, your favorite little granddaughter, gets sick, very sick, and you remember all of the other children who died before they could grow up, and you are very sad, because your granddaughter may be next. But the strange men send their "doctor", who gives your beautiful granddaughter some medicine, and in a few days she is up and running around with the other children.

After a year, the strange men tell you that they have defeated their enemy, and they begin to pack up their cargo, and some of them leave. But a new man arrives. This man is dressed differently, and he is not a warrior, but calls himself a "minister." He speaks your language well, which surprises everyone. And he begins to tell you about a new god, a god called Jesus, who came to Earth to save everyone from a terrible death. This minister tells you about heaven and hell, and it is very frightening.

Not only does the minister say that Jesus is God, but he also says that the other gods, the ones you and your ancestors have always worshipped, are false gods, that you must not worship your old gods any more, that you will surely go to hell if you don't accept this new Jesus god.

Many in the village do not believe the new minister. They have never heard of this Jesus before. But, it is very hard to understand – if your old gods were so powerful, why do these strange men, and their minister, have so much cargo, and such good medicine? Why was their doctor able to save your granddaughter? Maybe you should listen to this minister, and start praying to this Jesus god, for he must be a very powerful god indeed to have given such great riches, technology and medicine to these strange men.

The story related above is fictional, but it could be real – many such events actually happened. The "cargo cults" went much further than the tale above; there are documented cases where the natives tried to emulate western technology by building "radio towers" of bamboo, and clearing strips in the forest for the airplanes to land, in the hope of calling down more cargo from the sky.

The point we are interested in is not the cargo cult itself, but rather the legitimacy that western technology lends to the Religion Virus. The technological advances that took place between the Middle Ages and the twentieth century were a towering achievement of the collective minds of the human race. By the time of the colonial era, European technology, agriculture, and medicine were more advanced than every culture they encountered. Native people couldn't help but be impressed by huge ships, guns, steel knives, written language, woven clothes, glass, flint-and-steel fire starters, and hundreds of other cultural and technological wonders. Combine this with the idea, shared by almost all religions, that good things are granted to us by our gods, and you get a wide-open door for the introduction of Christianity.

Even though these "primitive" people weren't as technically advanced, they weren't stupid. They immediately recognized the value of Western technology, and were very impressed with the Europeans. Cargo cults are an of an extreme example, one in which a highly advanced technological culture suddenly "dumps" itself and all of its wonders into the midst of a technologically primitive society. But even in less extreme cases, relatively simple technology, such as glass beads, knives and axes, hand-held telescopes, and even sugar, had the power to impress less-advanced people. Missionaries were happy to "piggyback" on technology, gaining stature and legitimacy by their close association with the technology. It is best expressed as, "Your god is very good to you, he must be stronger than our old gods, so we'll listen to what you are teaching."

Religion and Military Technology

When the missionaries came to Africa they had the Bible and we had the land. They said, "Let us pray." We closed our eyes. When we opened them we had the Bible and they had the land.
– Desmond Tutu

Cargo cults illustrate that technology lent credibility to Western religions, Christianity in particular. The darker side of technology's role in the spread of Christianity is the advantage it gave in warfare.

One of the darkest days in the history of Western imperialism was November 16, 1532, when the Spanish explorer Pizarro, and a small force of just 168 soldiers, captured the Inca monarch Atahuallpa through dishonesty and guile, and then massacred over 7,000 Inca warriors, without a single Spanish death. The slaughter that day was stunning – *each* Spanish soldier must have hacked something like fifty Inca warriors to death with his sword. And 7,000 dead Incas doesn't tell the full story, because Atahualpa's army, which eventually fled in panic and disarray, was estimated at 80,000 Inca warriors.

Although guns played a role in the battle, the guns of that time were awkward and hard to reload, and Pizarro only had a dozen of them. Most of the military advantage was due to the Spaniards' steel swords, chain mail, and horses. An armored Spaniard on a horse with a sharp sword and steel lance was a pure killing machine, virtually invulnerable against the Incas' blunt clubs.

Pizarro's overwhelming victory is sometimes attributed to the fear and confusion that guns, horses, and a couple of horns blasting, caused among the Incas, and their surprise and fear at encountering them for the first time. But later battles with the Incas, and similar victories by Cortez against the Aztec warriors, proved that European technology, not the elements of surprise and fear, were responsible for the Spaniards' victories. Again and again, the Spaniards were victorious in massively lopsided battles. Small bands of a few dozen or a few hundred Spanish soldiers were consistently victorious against massively larger Inca and Aztec armies, even when these armies were well acquainted with the Spaniards' horses and guns.

Guns, Germs and Steel

Infectious diseases introduced [into America] with Europeans ... spread from one Indian tribe to another, far in advance of Europeans themselves, and killed an estimated 95% of the New World's Indian population.
– Jared Diamond

Cargo Cults demonstrate how technology can lend credibility to religion, and Pizarro's defeat of Atahuallpa illustrates how religion was aided by technology's contribution to military conquest. This leads us directly to the question: Why was Western technology so much superior to the rest of the world? Why did Western civilization and culture invade and dominate the rest of the world? Is there something about Western Europeans that made them superior to other races? Were they smarter, or harder working, or physically superior? Did they just get lucky? Or (some might ask) is there really a God who favored the Christians over all others? Why did the Westerners end up ahead of everyone else, and why did they end up colonizing a huge part of the world, spreading their culture, language, and religion at the expense of so many other cultures that were wiped out or severely diluted?

The title of this section, and the topics in it, are borrowed from and a tribute to Jared Diamond's book, *Guns, Germs and Steel*. Diamond's book answers these questions convincingly. If you had to boil down Diamonds entire book to a simple explanation, it would be this:

Westerners got lucky!

In other words, there was nothing magical about the rise and dominance of Western culture and its spread; rather, it was nothing more than good luck with the geography, climate, biodiversity, weather, livestock and diseases, that made Western culture advance faster and farther than other cultures.

I will make an attempt, in a few pages, to summarize and explain some of the insights that Diamond lays out. This is by no means a comprehensive summary of Diamond's insights, and any mistakes in this section are my own.

Below is a summary of the main factors in Western society's good luck.

Domestic Animals. Or more accurately, *domesticatable* animals. We're accustomed to horses, cows, pigs, and sheep, dogs and cats, and most of us never wonder where they came from. Why didn't the Australians or Native Americans have their own domestic animals? It was just bad luck. Diamond identifies six traits that an a domestic animal *cannot* have; any one of these traits makes the animal unsuitable for farming.

> *Nasty temper.* No matter how much contact it has with humans, an American buffalo will try to kill you if it can. An African zebra will do the same. A full-grown male ostrich can and will kill you with a single kick if you're not careful. No amount of breeding has helped, and these animals remain mostly non-domestic.

Panics easily. Open-plains herbivores tend to be the dinner of lions and hyenas. To survive, they've evolved a hair-trigger panic reaction, and they can run *fast*. How do you domesticate a gazelle that is terrified if you so much as sneeze, and then easily jumps a twenty-foot fence?

Grows slowly. Galapagos tortoises wouldn't be a good farm animal, because it would take longer than your lifetime for them to reach the age where you could eat them!

Picky eater. Panda bears only eat bamboo. They can't be raised anywhere their bamboo doesn't grow.

Won't breed in captivity. Some animal's mating rituals involve scenery or activities that they just can't do in a barn. You can't breed American Bald Eagles in captivity because their mating involves elaborate aerial displays, swoops and cartwheels, and locking talons in a freefall "wrestle" that only ends when the pair are about to hit the ground. Without this pre-mating rituals, the birds just don't get "in the mood for love."

Can't be dominated by humans. Animals like dogs already have a strong social structure, and if raised with humans will naturally accept humans as the "big dog." The "loner" animals are hard to domesticate.

In addition, domestic animals have to be the right size for working or for eating. You might be able to farm mice, but it's a lot of work to get enough mouse-meat for a meal.

When you take all of this into account, it turns out that, just by luck, almost all of the domesticatable animals happened to be in Eurasia. Cattle, sheep, pigs, chickens and horses are among the world's best domestic animals, and they're all from Eurasia. Africa had a few such as cattle, Central America had the llama and alpaca. North America had nothing decent to domesticate, so Native Americans had to resort to hunting the wild buffalo and deer, and Australia had a similar situation. Diamond gives an excellent and comprehensive accounting of every possible domesticatable animal in the world, and shows that the Europeans got almost all the luck.

Geography. Europeans also benefitted enormously from geographical luck: The Eurasian continent stretches across 173 degrees of longitude, nearly half way around the Northern Hemisphere, measuring roughly 12,000 kilometers east-to-west. This means that climate zones – the region where animals and crops can thrive – are huge. A horse could wander from Portugal on the Atlantic coast, to China on the Pacific coast, and find suitable weather and food the whole way. This gave Europeans a much wider ecological area to draw from for their domestic animals and crops.

By contrast, the Americas span a similar distance, but in the north-south direction. The Americas span roughly 125 degrees of latitude, from the Arctic almost to the Antarctic, yet the climate zones rarely span more than a few thousand kilometers in the east/west direction, and more often are less than 1000 kilometers. These relatively small ecological zones naturally have fewer species than the huge zones that span Eurasia. More importantly, the east/west climate zones form barriers to the north-south migration of species. For example, the Sonoran desert that spans northern Mexico and the American Southwest completely stops tropical plants and animals from crossing from Central America to North America. Many plants and animals from South and Central America could thrive in North America, but they never crossed the Sonoran desert.

Diseases. We've all heard of bird flu and swine flu, and that AIDS probably came from primates in Africa. It turns out that most deadly human diseases, such as measles, smallpox, and influenza, originate in animals and "jump" from our domestic animals to humans through close contact and chance mutation. Once again, Europeans "had all the luck." The horses, sheep, cows, chicken and sheep that the Europeans domesticated gave the Europeans lots of diseases. Plenty of Europeans died from these diseases, but more importantly, they developed immunity or resistance to them. By contrast, on continents where there were few or no domestic animals, there were also far fewer communicable diseases, and no immunity. When the disease-infested Europeans came into contact with the native people of the Americas, the Pacific Islands, Australia and New Zealand, disease transfer was almost exclusively one way: European diseases wiped out the native populations.

Nathaniel Philbrick's excellent history, *Mayflower*, chronicles the journey of America's first successful European settlers (the "Pilgrims") to America, and how they established their first town. Philbrick describes the typical outcome of contact between Europeans and natives:

> *The biggest advantage of the [Plymouth] area was that it had already been cleared by the Indians. And yet, nowhere could they find evidence of any recent Native settlements. The Pilgrims saw the eerie vacancy of this place as a miraculous gift from God... Just three years before... there had been between one thousand and two thousand people living along these shores ... the banks of the harbor had been dotted with wigwams, each with a curling plume of wood smoke... and with fields of corn, beans and squash growing nearby. Dugout canoes ... plied the waters. ... Then, from 1616 to 1619, disease brought this centuries-old community to an end. [By] the winter of 1620, gruesome evidence of the epidemic was scattered all around the area. "[T]heir skulls and bones were found in many places lying still above the ground...," Bradford wrote, "a very sad spectacle to behold." It was here, on the bone-whitened hills of Plymouth, that the pilgrims hoped to begin a new life.*

The Pilgrims' experience was the rule rather than the exception. Everywhere Europeans went, their diseases caused staggering death rates: fifty percent, eighty percent, even ninety-nine percent of indigenous people would die.

Farmable Crops. Again, just by luck, Eurasia had almost all of the farmable crops in the world, and had a climate suitable for developing agriculture. We all learned in grammar school about the *Fertile Crescent*, which stretches from Egypt, through Israel and

Lebanon, on to parts of Jordan, Syria, Iraq, south-eastern Turkey and ends with south-western Iran. The Fertile Crescent was more than just conducive to farming, it also just happened to have a number of wild grains (such as wheat) that were suitable for domestication. By bad luck, no other continent had more than a few crops suitable for farming.

In America, only a very few plants such as corn, beans and squash could be farmed. The grains in America were uniformly unsuitable – the grain was too small, and a crop produced very little usable food. American agriculture was also hindered by geography: The Americas span a huge distance north-to-south, whereas Eurasia spans a huge distance east to west. Without no extensive long-range trading between the peoples of North and South America, a crop that might be farmable in South America had little chance of crossing the tropics, then crossing the Sonoran desert, to a farmer in North America. By contrast, a crop that grows well in China can find its way across the continent to Europe, since there is a climatic zone suitable for the crop that spans the whole continent.

Another barrier to domestication of crops is that a farming society needs more than one crop to sustain it. American Indians domesticated corn and squash, but they still had to hunt and fish, and a full farming economy never developed. Again, Eurasia had all the luck: The many domesticatable plants made a variety of crops possible, which was the foundation of a full farming economy.

We can hardly do justice to Professor Diamond's 480-page Pulitzer-Prize winning book *Guns, Germs and Steel* in just a few pages of this book, but I hope I have conveyed enough of his thesis to illustrate the main point: The rise of Western culture and technology were largely due to accidental circumstances. The Christians just happened to live on the right continent.

The Synergy of Religion, Technology and Government

> *It has been the scheme of the Christian Church, and of all*
> *the other invented systems of religion, to hold man in igno-*
> *rance of the Creator, as it is of Governments to hold man in*
> *ignorance of his rights. The systems of the one are as false*
> *as those of the other, and are calculated for mutual support.*
> *– Thomas Paine (1737-1809)*

The story of the Israelites' return to their "promised land" is one of the traditional high points in Jewish history. Yahweh, after letting the Israelites wander through the desert for generations, and suffer all sorts of indignities and defeats at the hands of their enemies, finally brought them "home" to the land of Canaan, and miraculously felled the walls of Jericho. This land, "overflowing with milk and honey," was given as Yahweh's reward to the Jews.

But this "milk and honey" didn't spring from the ground; the land Yahweh was turning over to the Israelites already belonged to someone else, the Canaanites, who had worked hard to make it a wonderful land. There is a saying, "history is written by the victors," so we don't have the Canaanite's side of this tale. But it's a good bet they would portray the Israelites as heartless murderers. The Israelites, with Yahweh's permission, "... devoted to destruction by the edge of the sword all in the city, both men and women, young and old, oxen, sheep and donkeys."

Most readers (Christians and Jews) of this story unconsciously identify with the victors; after all, who likes a loser? This leads to a conqueror mentality, a belief that God is on the side of the winner. And it wasn't just in war – In most European nations, aristocracy and royalty put forth the idea that their exalted positions were a sign of God's approval. On a national level, whole countries believed the same thing: European colonial nations were successful in their imperialist expansions because God approved, and was helping them take God's words to the non-Christian nations. They wore a "mantle of Jericho," justifying their conquests with the belief that it was their *duty* to dominate and enlighten the less advanced people they conquered. You can't just steal your neighbor's farm and cows without a good excuse, and you can't just invade a neighboring country (or one half way around the globe) without a reason. Jericho was that reason.

A new school of thought called "post-colonial theology" takes a more balanced view of the Bible, trying to see events such as the fall of Jericho from both sides. The falling walls of Jericho were the Israelites' miracle, and the Canaanites' catastrophe. Yahweh's gift of the Promised Land to the Israelites was simple thievery to the Canaanites. The Israelites' victory was the Canaanites' genocide. The prostitute Rahab, who hid Joshua's spies, was a hero to the Israelites, but a vile traitor to the Canaanites.

This same more enlightened attitude is being applied to all aspects of our history. Pizarro's massacre of the Incas is just one example where a post-colonial attitude helps us see the conquest from both points of view. Pizarro, in addition to being a Spanish hero, is also a vile liar, a dishonest man who lured an Inca monarch into a trap with dishonorable lies, and then massacred over 7,000 Incas (including hundreds of non-combatants) in a single day, stopping only when darkness brought a halt to his crimes.

When we add the insights of Diamond's *Guns, Germs and Steel*, the story is even more clear. Pizarro was simply wrong when he claimed God was on his side. It wasn't Yahweh that sided with Western imperialism to help spread Christianity. God didn't have anything to do with it. Geographical accidents helped Western culture develop faster. The Religion Virus partnered with technology and government and thereby vastly increased its hold on human society. Pizarro was nothing more than a thief and murderer, killing for profit.

Christianity spread through sheer good luck: It happened that Jesus was born on the right continent, nothing more.

Interlude: Aunt Carolyn's Un-Baptism

I do not feel obliged to believe that that same God who has
endowed us with sense, reason, and intellect has intended us
to forgo their use.
– Galileo Galilei (1564-1642)

It was my father's death that triggered the writing of this book.
He lived to be almost eighty, but he might have lived to one hundred
but for some bad luck.

During World War II, Dad and his buddy "Doug" (not his real
name) got weekend leave from the US Army, and they jumped on
Dad's big, powerful Indian motorcycle to head home (Doug was
driving, Dad on the back). Coming down California's Central
Valley, State Highway 33 is completely flat for hundreds of miles,
from way up north in Yarmouth near the San Joaquin River, for 215
miles south until you get to McKittrick, just before Highway 33
heads into the Santa Ynez Mountains. Flat, that is, except for one
hill, near the town of Westley. Just one. And for some reason on
that fateful night, Doug decided to pass a slow-moving truck as they
crested the only hill on that road.

As Doug pulled around the truck and crested the hill, another
motorcycle appeared dead ahead, coming up the other side. For
some crazy reason, Doug panicked and swerved to the *left* side of the
oncoming motorcycle. Of course, the oncoming motorcyclist
swerved the same way. Just before the collision, both drivers locked
their rear wheels in a skid, and the two motorcycles slammed into
each other at a combined speed of around one hundred miles per
hour, crushing all three riders' right legs between the heavy
machines.

A couple hours later, my Dad woke up, lying in a farmer's field.
A hundred yards off, he could see an ambulance, tow truck, various
police cars, and people milling about. He called out and yelled, and
after a while someone noticed him. They were stunned – they'd
found two motorcycles, and two motorcyclists, and thought that was

it. Later when he returned to the site, he estimated that he must have flown clear over the telephone wires and the railroad track to have landed so far away. His leg was broken in seventeen places, his knee completely smashed, and he had various other broken ribs and injuries. But he was alive.

The accident sent him to the hospital for over year, and left him with a shattered knee, no kneecap, and a terrible and (at the time) incurable bone infection (osteomyelitis). He later had three full artificial knee replacements, none of which really worked well, which meant he never exercised at all. This, combined with fifty years of smoking and a diet high in salami, cheese on crackers, and fried chicken, meant that the natural robustness and longevity that runs in my family was truncated. He might have lived a full century, but instead became feeble and disabled in his early seventies and died six months short of his eightieth birthday.

Aunt Carolyn (my father's sister) has the same strong constitution as my father, but she is as robust as can be – she's just one year younger than my father, and at age seventy-eight, she was a volunteer who drove her own car to the very same retirement home where my father spent his last months, to play piano and sing for the "old folks."

Death is never easy, even when you're ready for it and know it will bring peace. Aunt Carolyn offered me a bed to sleep in and a shoulder to cry on during the last few difficult months of of my father's life, when I had to travel frequently to take care of him. Her calm, loving care and restful home were a refuge, but most of all, she knew when to just listen. After I'd unloaded my frustrations each evening, Aunt Carolyn and I had some wonderful late-night discussions about everything from politics, to the morality of family assisted suicide, to the existence of God.

You may recall from my story, Grandpa and the Sunset, that I come from a very religious family on my father's side, and that included Aunt Carolyn. So you can imagine my surprise and amazement to find that Aunt Carolyn, who had been Christian most of her life, had done a 180-degree turn late in life and become an atheist. I found this fascinating, but with my father's death shortly after this conversation, I had many things to take care of. I bid Aunt Carolyn farewell and headed home. That was in January.

July thirty-first would have been Dad's eightieth birthday, and I decided to call Aunt Carolyn to reconnect. We started talking about religion again, and I asked her about her "un-baptism" – her conversion from Christianity to something close to atheism. Her story might be described as "typical" except for the ending.

The first crack in her faith was during her teen years when she learned the horrors of Hitler and his genocide of the Jews and Gypsies. Aunt Carolyn couldn't understand how the loving god Jehovah could let such a thing happen. Her path continued in the usual way, with unanswered prayers, consternation over all the weird conflicts and inconsistencies in the Bible that nobody could explain to her satisfaction, and with her recognizing the staggering cruelty, horrifying natural disasters, and so forth, that are hard to explain if God is the kind and loving God she learned about in church. But she tried to keep her faith, although it was difficult, for several more decades.

In the 1970s, Aunt Carolyn decided she really, truly wanted to have her faith back, and she recommitted herself to Christianity and Jesus. In 1984, she joined the Episcopal Church, where she spent almost five years studying and trying to reconcile the church's teachings with the reality she found all around her. It almost worked.

Her faith in God ended utterly and completely in one single day. Aunt Carolyn had the opportunity to travel extensively in South and Central America as the wife of an American diplomat. She happened to be in Peru and Ecuador when a volcano erupted. Lava, mud and ashes cascaded down its slopes, killing and destroying everything in its path. One man became trapped in the mud, stuck up to his shoulders, unable to move. They couldn't free him.

Buried alive, but able to breath, he screamed for mercy, begging the Catholic priest to kill him, or let his friends or family do it. The priest, all the people in the village, and the man himself, knew with certainty that he was going to die. Yet the priest refused, for to kill the man would be a mortal sin. It was God's will, that this man had to die of "natural" causes, even if that meant days and days of insufferable torture. The man screamed and begged, but the villagers, all Catholics, would not go against the priest's command. The man finally died in pain and agony.

When Aunt Carolyn heard this story, her faith evaporated in a single day. In that moment, she finally realized that the answer to her long quest had been in front of her the whole time: There is no God.

The genesis of this book came during my late-night discussions with Aunt Carolyn before Dad died, when she asked me about my own beliefs. Having heard about her "un-baptism," I was encouraged to tell her my own theories. Somehow, in about five minutes, I gave Aunt Carolyn an unbelievably lucid and succinct explanation of these ideas. It was one of those moments that I wish I had recorded, because I'll probably never be that concise and clear again. But that moment inspired me – I realized that all these ideas had finally come together in my head, and it was time to write this book.

And here it is. Thanks, Aunt Carolyn, for taking care of me, thanks for asking about my beliefs, and thanks for listening while I talked nonstop for five minutes. I can't tell you how much your story has inspired me.

And thanks for taking me into your home and heart in my time of need.

religion into the incredibly powerful and attractive Religion Virus that it is today.

Memes, like living lifeforms, are in constant competition with one another for survival. This book is my small contribution to the battle: I hope that I've created an anti-religion memeplex, a sort of "inoculation" against the Religion Virus. The goal which I share with many atheists, and also many Deists and thoughtful members of many of the newer liberal churches, is to clear the ideosphere of the harmful religion viruses that plague modern humankind. By exposing the roots of the religion virus, my hope is to weaken its grip on humanity.

All species are affected by changes in their environment, and the religion virus is no exception. As technology unraveled many of the mysteries of the universe, religion lost some of its power. The religion virus' ecology is becoming more hostile. I hope that, in some small way, I've made its environment even more hostile, so that the religion virus will have fewer minds to infect.

Acknowledgements

Several people read the early drafts, for which I am deeply grateful.

Brian McGoldrick, Phil Steele, Leo James, Karen Calcagno, Jessica Smith, Carolyn Buxton ("Aunt Carolyn") and Matt Hahn all suffered through the early, deeply flawed drafts. Each one of them provided invaluable and detailed comments, criticism and advice, and a unique perspective on the book's contents. I am very grateful to each of you.

In addition to her editorial help, Carolyn Buxton also provided fascinating details about my family's history and, of course, the stories behind the *Interludes* about her "unbaptism" and my father's motorcycle accident.

I would like to give special mention to Professor Terry Winograd of Stanford University, who unknowingly contributed to this book. His brilliant lectures on linguistics, language, cognition, and the true meaning of human consciousness, started me down a path twenty-four years ago that ultimately lead to this book.

Finally, I must acknowledge the profound influence my father had on my views of religion, morality, humanity, and history. He taught me to question everything, to look at every topic from both sides, and to appreciate a good discussion. The word "thank" would be inappropriate here, for reasons my father knew all too well; a simple acknowledgement is what he would have expected.

Bibliography

BOOKS:

Darwin, Charles (1872). *The Origin of the Species (sixth edition)*. New York: Singet.

Dawkins, Richard (2006). *The God Delusion*. Boston, New York: Houghton Mifflin Company.

Dawkins, Richard (1986). *The Blind Watchmaker*. New York: W. W. Norton and Company.

Dawkins, Richard (1976). *The Selfish Gene*. Oxford: Oxford University Press

Dawkins, Richard (2005). *The Ancestor's Tale*. Boston: Houghton Mifflin.

Dennett, Daniel C. (2006). *Breaking the Spell*. New York: Viking Penguin.

Dennett, Daniel C. (1995). *Darwin's Dangerous Idea: Evolution and the Meaning of Life*. New York: Touchstone.

Dennet, Daniel C. (1991). *Consciousness Explained*. New York: LIttle, Brown and Company.

Diamond, Jared (1999). *Guns, Germs and Steel: The Fates of Human Society*. New York: W. W. Norton & Company.

Diamond, Jared (2005). *Collapse: How Societies Choose to Fail or Succeed*. New York: Viking, The Penguin Group.

Durham, William H. (1991). *Coevolution: Genes, Culture, and Human Diversity*. Stanford University Press.

Ehrman, Bart D (2005). *Misquoting Jesus: The Story Behind Who Changed the Bible and Why*. New York: HarperCollins.

Garrison, Becky (2007). *The New Atheist Crusaders and Their Unholy Grail: The Misguided Quest to Destroy Your Faith*. Dallas: Thomas Nelson.

Gladwell, Malcolm (2002). *The Tipping Point: How Little Things Can Make a Big Difference*. New York: Back Bay Books / Little, Brown and Company.

Gould, Stephen Jay (1989). *Wonderful Life: The Burgess Shale and the Nature of History*. New York: W. W. Norton & Company.

Gould, Stephan Jay (1977). *Ever Since Darwin: Reflections on Natural History*. New York: W. W. Norton & Company.

Gould, Stephan Jay (1980). *The Panda's Thumb: More Reflections in Natural History*. New York: W. W. Norton & Company.

Gould, Stephan Jay (2002). *The Structure of Evolutionary Theory*. Cambridge, Massachusetts: Belknap Press.

Hamer, Dean and Copeland, Peter (1998). *Living With our Genes*. New York: Doubleday.

Harris, Sam (2005). *The End of Faith: Religion, Terror, and the Future of Reason*. New York: W. W. Norton & Company.

Hitchens, Christopher (2007). *God is Not Great: How Religion Poisons Everything*. New York: Twelve, Hachette Book Group USA.

Kelly, David (1986). *The Evidence of the Senses: A Realist Theory of Perception*. Louisiana State University Press.

Kirsch, Jonathan (2004). *God Against the Gods: The History of the War Between Monotheism and Polytheism*. New York: Viking Compass, the Penguin Group.

Kuhn, Thomas S. (1970). *The Structure of Scientific Revolutions (2nd edition)*. Chicago: University of Chicago Press.

Lamont, Corliss (1988). *The Philosophy of Humanism* (sixth edition). New York: The Continuum Publishing Company.

Lewis, David (1994). *We, the Navigators: The Ancient Art of Landfinding in the Pacific*. Honolulu: University of Hawaii Press.

March, Frederic (2006). *The Bible Through the Eyes of its Authors*. New York: iUniverse.

Mills, David (2006). *Atheist Universe: The Thinking Person's Answer to Christian Fundamentalism*. Berkeley: Ulysses Press.

Paulos, John Allen (2008). *Irreligion: A Mathematician Explains Why the Arguments for God Just Don't Add Up*. New York: Hill and Wang.

Philbrick, Nathaniel (2006) *Mayflower*. New York: Viking, The Penguin Group.

Russell, Bertrand. *Why I am Not a Christian and other essays on religion and related subjects*. Edited by Paul Edwards, 1957. New York: Simon and Schuster.

Wills, Christopher (1989). *The Wisdom of the Genes: New Pathways in Evolution*. New York: Basic Books.

– 198 –

SCIENTIFIC PAPERS:

The Amung Way: the Subsistence Strategies, the Knowledge and the Dilemma of the Tsinga Valley People in Irian Jaya, Indonesia. Cook, Carolyn Diane Turinsky (1995) PhD Dissertation, Southern Illinois University at Carbondale. http://www.papuaweb.org/dlib/s123/cook/_phd.html

Herrick's 1910 case report of sickle cell anemia. The rest of the story. Journal of the American Medical Association, 1989 Jan 13;261(2):266-71.

Vichinsky, Elliott P., M.D. *Pulmonary Hypertension in Sickle Cell Disease.* The New England Journal of Medicine, 2004 Feb 26; Number 9, Volume 350:857-859

Goodall, J. 1977. *Infant Killing and Cannabalism in Free-living Chimpanzees.* Folia Primatologica. Vol. 28, 259-282. (As cited on http://www.primates.com/chimps/chimpanzee-info.html)

WEB RESOURCES:

History of Judaism, Christianity, Islam, and much, much more ...
http://www.wikipedia.com/

Online Searchable Bible, many editions:
http://www.biblegateway.com/

The Catholic Encyclopedia:
http://www.catholic.org/encyclopedia/

The Skeptics Annotated Bible:
http://skepticsannotatedbible.com

Religions in the United States, from the CIA Factbook:
https://www.cia.gov/library/publications/the-world-factbook/geos/us.html

William Paley, Cicery quote:
http://en.wikipedia.org/wiki/Watchmaker_analogy

John Morris quote, from Institute for Creation Research:
http://www.icr.org/articles/print/1078/

History of Papua New Guinea:
http://www.geographia.com/papua-newguinea/papuahistory.htm
http://en.wikipedia.org/wiki/New_Guinea

Who was the First Observed Sickle-Cell Patient?
www.nslc.wustl.edu/sicklecell/part1/noel.pdf (No author listed in PDF file)

Hayes, Diana. 1998. *Reflections on Slavery,* in Curran, Charles E. *Change in Official Catholic Moral Teaching*, as quoted in Wikipedia, http://en.wikipedia.org/wiki/Dum_Diversas

Coca Cola song:
http://en.wikipedia.org/wiki/I'd_Like_to_Teach_the_World_to_Sing

Zeus and Jupiter:
http://www.nowpublic.com/culture/zeus-or-jupiter-last-you-know-difference

The Evolution of Language.
http://library.thinkquest.org/C004367/la1.shtml

Article on *Biblical Inerrancy*, by Stephen L. Andrew.
Chaffer Theological Seminary Journal, volume 8, number 1.
http://www.chafer.edu/journal/back_issues/v8n1_1.pdf

Index